DYBBUKS
and Jewish Women
in Social History,
Mysticism and Folklore

DYBBUKS
and Jewish Women
in Social History, Mysticism and Folklore

RACHEL ELIOR

URIM PUBLICATIONS
Jerusalem • New York

Dybbuks and Jewish Women in Social History, Mysticism and Folklore
by Rachel Elior
Translated from the Hebrew by Joel Linsider.

Originally published in Hebrew as the following:

"*Ha-dibbuk: bein ha-olam ha-nigleh la-olam ha-nistar: Kolot medaberim, olamot shotekim ve-kolot mushtakim.*" In *Derekh ha-ruah: sefer ha-yovel le-Eliezer Schweid.* Edited by Yehoyada Amir, 499–536. Jerusalem: Van Leer Institute, 2005.

"*Kemo Sophia, Marcelle ve-Lizzie.*" *Kivunim hadashim* 17 (2007): 144–163.

Printed in Israel. First Edition.
Layout design by Satya Levine.
ISBN: 978-965-524-007-8

Urim Publications
P.O. Box 52287, Jerusalem 91521 Israel

Lambda Publishers Inc.
3709 13th Avenue Brooklyn, New York 11218 U.S.A.
Tel: 718-972-5449 Fax: 718-972-6307, mh@ejudaica.com

www.UrimPublications.com

This book is dedicated to the memory of my beloved parents, courageous proponents of compassion, devotion and freedom: my father, Shmuel Palagee (1911–1981) and my mother, Leah Palagee (1912–2002). The book is further dedicated to the memory of my beloved friends who drew my attention to the lives of people who were living between two worlds in more than one way: Orna Zohar-Rottblit (1945–1998), Ariella Deem-Goldberg (1934–1985), Sari Foierstein (1945–1979) and Enid Soifer-McKenna (1943–2007).

CONTENTS

Preface

This book includes two essays. The opening essay, "Like Sophia and Marcelle and Lizzie," discusses general issues pertaining to Jewish women in the traditional patriarchal society through various historical periods. The second essay, "Speaking Voices, Silencing Worlds, Silenced Voices," elaborates on a particular topic, the *dybbuk*, which reflects a unique feminine response to the constraints of the dominant masculine order.

"Speaking Voices, Silencing Worlds, Silenced Voices" rests on the premise that every socio-cultural-historical concept that is preserved in language and that recurs in a stereotypical literary, interpretive and textual construct entails numerous levels of meaning, implicitly and explicitly revealed and transmitted by diverse voices. In this inquiry into the meaning of the dybbuk, my aim is to introduce into the chorus of scholarly voices on the subject – voices on which this essay is based and to which it owes a debt of gratitude – some hitherto silenced voices and marginalized perspectives. These voices are brought to the fore in the context of a gender-based reading of the suppressed linguistic meanings of the terms analyzed here. Language, which embodies social values and preserves thought constructs and ways of life, allows for the examination from various perspectives of the relationship between the language preserved in literature and drama and the concrete or imaginative reality it reflects.

Professors Yoram Bilu and Gedaliah Nigal have done fundamental work on the dybbuk in Jewish culture, and their studies have been of great value in my work here. But the interpretive point of departure that I want to present differs from theirs, for it pertains to the gender-based perspective on the issue and to its social meaning as tied to the kabbalistic tradition.

My thanks to my student, Dr. Rivka Devir-Goldberg, who assisted me in gathering the material discussed here and elucidating the early stages of the study in the mid-1990s. Many thanks to Joel Linsider for his expert translation of both essays from the original Hebrew into English, and to David Friedman, a devoted friend, who helped me to improve the style and content of the English version of old Hebrew texts presented in these essays. Heartfelt thanks to my dear friend, Leona Rosenberg, who helped me through her generosity to conclude the latter stages of this work. Lastly, I wish to thank the Memorial Foundation for Jewish Culture for supporting the research for these essays, and Felix Posen and the Posen Foundation for their generous support.

Note on Translations

In "Like Sophia and Marcelle and Lizzie," Hebrew Bible quotations are from the old Jewish Publication Society (OJPS) translation (Philadelphia: Jewish Publication Society of America, 1917 [1958 printing].) Apocrypha and New Testament quotations are from the New Revised Standard Version Bible (NRSV), copyright © 1989 by the Division of Christian Education of the National Council of the Churches of Christ in the U.S.A., and are used by permission. All rights reserved.

In "Speaking Voices, Silencing Worlds, Silenced Voices," unattributed translations of primary sources and Hebrew secondary sources are by the present translator. Hebrew Bible translations are from the new Jewish Publication Society version (NJPS), Tanakh, (Philadelphia: Jewish Publication Society of America, 1999).

"Like Sophia and Marcelle and Lizzie"

> The woman, says the Law, is in all things inferior to the man. Let her accordingly be submissive, not for her humiliation, but that she may be directed; for the authority has been given by God to the man.
>
> Josephus Flavius, *Against Apion* 2:24

In an interview published about eight years ago, Israeli writer Dorit Rabinyan, born in 1972, incisively described the anguish of the women among whom she had grown up: "Like Sophia, Marcelle, and Lizzie, lest they remain in a position of limited possibilities, constrained initiative, and attenuated will."[1]

The question I want to consider is whether a position of limited possibilities, constrained initiative, and attenuated will were the lot of women only in particular communities or whether they were the fate of most women until the second half of the twentieth century. Let me say at the outset that I am inclined toward the latter premise, for the historical record shows that the lot of most women in most places was aptly

---

[1] Interview, *Yedi`ot Aḥronot*, March 1999.

characterized by the comments of Creon, King of Thebes: "Slaves, bring them inside. The freedom of women must be constrained" (Sophocles, *Antigone* 578–580[2]). Moreover, it seems to me that Tolstoy's famous remark in the Introduction to *Anna Karenina* – "All happy families resemble one another; every unhappy family is unhappy in its own way" – applies to our subject. At all times and in all communities, happy women have resembled one another in that freedom of choice, a life of liberty, freedom of speech, and multiple possibilities were available to them to a greater or lesser degree, such that they were able to live their lives as they wished within the bounds of their communities. On the other hand, those who suffered coercion, rejection, discrimination, inferiority, stigmatization, silence and enslavement were unhappy in all places and at all times. The possibility of choice and a degree of freedom were available to men and women to different degrees in various places by virtue of love of parents, familial brotherhood, marital love, or love of children. The select, fortunate few might also attain a degree of freedom by force of their intellect or through customary practices that enabled the subjugated to free themselves from the oppressive social order. For the most part, however, it was a patriarchal social order in which all institutions, from family to government, were led by men. Women were prevented from raising their voices and participating in any communal arena involving intellect, influence, teaching, justice, law, liberty, or authority.

From time to time, individual women could dare to shape their lives as they chose. These fortunate few benefited from love, wisdom, knowledge, justice, tolerance, cooperation, freedom, or equality within the bounds of happy families. But unfortunate women in all communities suffered lives of coercion and misery, of limited possibilities, constrained initiative,

---

[2] English based on the Hebrew translation by Aaron Shabtai (Tel Aviv: Schocken 1990), 56.

silenced voices and attenuated free will. The men of their families and their communities subjected them to constraints, coercion, discrimination, marginalization, ignorance, silence and rejection; they did so by force of ancient laws, ancestral customs, changing rules, governmental decrees, and powerful myths that traced the lowly state of women to the beginning of time. The regnant patriarchal worldview regarding male-female power relationships is concisely summed up in the words of Josephus Flavius, the first-century C.E. Jewish historian. Josephus, commander of the Jewish fortress of Yodfat (Jotapata) during the war against the Romans, betrayed his command and went over to the Roman side, later living in Rome under the shelter of the imperial family and writing there in an effort to explain the Torah and the Jewish point of view to the Gentiles. The worldview he describes grounds its explicit authority and implicit utility in a divine source that cannot be disputed and that precludes its implicit human purposes:

> The woman, says the Law, is in all things inferior to the man. Let her accordingly be submissive, not for her humiliation, but that she may be directed; for the authority has been given by God to the man.[3]

Josephus's contemporary, the Jewish Pharisee Saul of Tarsus – later known as Paul – developed this position further. The New Testament includes his statement reflecting the widespread viewpoint in the Jewish world of his day, which connected mythological stories with concrete punishments of exclusion and silencing: "Let a woman learn in silence with full submission. I permit no woman to teach or to have authority over a

---

[3] *Against Apion*, 2:24, trans. H. St. J. Thackeray (Loeb Classical Library) (London: Wm. Heineman; New York: G. P. Putnam's Sons, 1926), vol. 1, 373.

man; she is to keep silent. For Adam was formed first, then Eve; and Adam was not deceived, but the woman was deceived and became a transgressor. Yet she will be saved through childbearing, provided they continue in faith and love and holiness, with modesty."[4]

Until the twentieth century, all Jewish communities lived, to one degree or another, under the patriarchal order reflected in the words of Josephus Flavius and Saul of Tarsus. Men enjoyed exclusive authority over knowledge, government, public discourse, and law and had the exclusive power to shape the public arena, for they were regarded by their very nature as pure beings able to draw near to holiness and learning and to become scholars. Women, meanwhile, occupied a secondary position – socially inferior, denied a public voice, excluded from the circle of scholars, maintained in ignorance, and legally discriminated against – for they were regarded as periodically impure by reason of their menstrual cycles, which excluded them from holiness and study.[5] Women, like men, internalized the array of beliefs and opinions that portrayed women as inferior, impure, sinful, guilty and punished, ignorant, and subjugated to their fathers and their husbands – a situation going back to the time the spokesmen for the patriarchal order linked a mythological sin (Eve's

---

[4] 1 Timothy 2:11–15 (NRSV).

[5] See Rachel Elior, "'*Nokheḥot nifkadot,' 'teva domem,' ve-'almah yafah she-ein lah einayim': li-she'elat nokheḥutan ve-he`adran shel nashim, bi-leshon ha-kodesh, ba-dat ha-yehudit, u-ve-meẓi'ut ha-yisra'elit*" [On the question of women's presence and absence in the Hebrew language, the Jewish religion, and Israeli society], *Alpayyim* 20 (2000): 214–270 [portions translated into English by Rachelle Avital as "'Present but Absent,' 'Still Life' and 'A Pretty Maiden Who Has No Eyes': On the Presence and Absence of Women in the Hebrew Language, in Jewish Culture and in Israeli Life," in *Streams Into the Sea: Studies in Jewish Culture and Its Context, Dedicated to Felix Posen,* edited by Elḥanan Reiner and Rachel Livneh-Freudenthal, 191–211. Tel Aviv: Alma, 2001.

dealings with the snake) to concrete punishments ("and he shall rule over thee"; Gen. 3:16) that gave rise to the conventional social order and the power relationships between rulers and ruled. Moreover, the overseers of these arrangements intimidated women through a system that would brand anyone who dissented from the patriarchal order, or even criticized it, as a rebel, a whore, a harlot, a traitor, or a deviant. In this way, there emerged a situation in which women (impure, silent, and ignorant by reason of being removed from sanctity and knowledge) were subservient to men (pure and learned, near to holiness and study, publicly vocal) in many areas, both external and internal. They were denied access to many sorts of knowledge, their entry into the study hall was forbidden, their entry into the synagogue was limited, and they were required to maintain complete silence in the public domain.[6] They were entirely dependent on those who possessed knowledge and wealth, and their fathers and husbands exercised nearly absolute dominion over them. A woman was under her father's authority until she married, at which time she passed to the dominion of the husband who had acquired her from her father ("A woman is acquired in [any of] three ways" [*Mishnah Kiddushin* 1:1]). Women at a very early age – girls, really – were given in marriages arranged by their families and were denied economic independence or sovereign status. They were unable to approach the circles of study, sanctity, and authority; and they were destined

[6] An instructive example of the link between the labeling of women as menstrually impure (the Hebrew word for which, *niddah*, is related to the word for banishment) and their total exclusion from the synagogue can be found in *Baraita de-masekhet niddah* (ed. Horowitz) (Frankfurt 1892): "It is forbidden for a menstruant to pray and to enter the synagogue" (Horowitz 3, 17). See *Eruvin* 100b on the link between Eve's sin and women's punishment.

primarily to marry young, serve their husbands, fulfill all their needs, and bear them children.[7]

Did women in certain communities necessarily suffer more than those in other communities? Were coerced marriages, or marriages arranged by parents for a girl of twelve, more difficult for a girl in Yemen than for one in Frankfurt? Was bearing children at age thirteen or fourteen easier for a girl in Frankfurt than for one in Aden? Did their ignorance distress women in Casablanca and in Venice to differing degrees? Did women in Vilna, Djerba, and Miedzyboz, in Dar`a and Sana`a have the same yearning to study? Did rape victims in Constantinople or Rabat suffer more than those in Moscow or Lodz? Were poverty and economic dependency more difficult for women in Zhitomir and Cracow than for those in Cairo and Baghdad? It appears that most women in all Jewish communities were entirely dependent economically on their husbands. That dependence was the consequence of the inheritance and property laws articulated in Scripture and *halakhah* (under which women did not share with their brothers in their fathers' estates), of the marriage laws detailed in those sources, and of the widespread norm and expectation that men would be scholars and women would support them in realizing that goal, which stood

---

[7] See Adiel Schremer, *Zakhar u-nekevah bera'am* [*Male and Female He Created Them*] [Marriage in the end of Second Temple period and in the talmudic era]. (Jerusalem: Merkaz Zalman Shazar, 2003). Marriage at an early age was common for women in the Hellenistic-Roman period in all Mediterranean societies; they were betrothed at around the age of twelve to men who were in their late twenties (id., 125, n. 66). A first marriage, commonly based on endogamy, was organized by the woman's parents (id., 136–142). On androcentrism in relation to marriage laws and its implications in late antiquity, see Shaye J.D. Cohen, *From the Maccabees to the Mishnah* (Westminster: John Knox Press, 2d ed., 1998), 70–73. In medieval and early modern Jewish society, marriage at an early age was common for Jewish men and women alike; see n. 12 below.

at the pinnacle of the community's value system. Scholarship, property ownership, and authoritative opinions were limited to men. Women acquiesced willy-nilly in the limitations imposed by the patriarchal order, given their ignorance, subservience, dependence, and downtrodden state, grounded both in *halakhah* and in the myth of Eve's sin and curse. All of these, together with the biological reality that left them as pregnant or nursing for a substantial part of their lives, starting at a very early age, kept them from protesting against these hallowed arrangements. But everywhere there were women who suffered intensely as a result of this corrupt order, with its grounding in sacred traditions and ancient myths; and they sought various ways, explicit and implicit, to free themselves from it.

By the nature of things, every human community operates in different cultural, political, geographical and historical circumstances. These depend on geographic reality and ambient social norms, on prevailing law and hallowed conventions; but the Torah is unique in casting the biological and psychological difference between the sexes as a punishment and in unambiguously declaring the power relationships between the sexes to be a divine curse: "I will greatly multiply thy pain and thy travail; in pain thou shalt bring forth children; and thy desire shall be to thy husband, and he shall rule over thee" (Gen. 3:16).[8] Alongside it, there developed the *halakhah*, which unequivocally declared the inferiority of women in all Jewish communities when it said, summarily, "A man has precedence over a woman with respect to saving a life" (*Mishnah Horayot* 3:7), adding "A man may divorce only if he wills it, but a woman may be divorced against her will as a matter of Torah [as distinct from rabbinic] law" (*Mishnah*

---

[8] Some ancient versions such as the Septuagint (third century B.C.E.), as well as the Book of Jubilees (second century B.C.E.) and the translation of the Torah into Ge'ez read "your turning" or "your accountability" (*teshuvatekh*) rather than "your desire (*teshukatekh*) shall be to your husband."

Yevamot 1:14). Common adages limited woman's capabilities to narrow areas: "There is no wisdom in women except at the spindle"; "Women's minds are frivolous"; "Do not converse excessively with women." These were connected to the blessing recited by men every morning in all Jewish communities; immediately after praising God for not having made him a slave, a man would praise God for not having made him a woman (*Tosefta Berakhot* 7:10, 18). All of these left their mark on the shared consciousness of gender-based superiority and inferiority and molded the male-female relationship as one of dominance and subjugation, sovereignty and dependence, enslavement and obedience, freedom to speak and obedient silence. This grim picture, of course, was not unique to rabbinic Judaism and was characteristic as well of the surrounding cultures that exercised considerable influence on how the rabbis and sages lived. Indeed, it would have been surprising had they acted against the contemporary mores of their time on this issue. It should be noted, moreover, that the rabbis expressed respect for obedient and diligent women within their families as daughters, sisters, wives and mothers and took various steps to ameliorate the condition of women – for example, by giving them some economic protection in the event of divorce. This favorable attention, however, was always limited to the private domain. Definitive halakhic statements exclude women from the seats of authority and judicial institutions ("A woman neither judges nor testifies" [*Yerushalmi Yoma* 6:1, 43b]); exclude them from the public domain generally ("A woman's voice is nakedness" [*Kiddushin* 70a]); consign women to ignorance forever throughout the Jewish world ("One who teaches his daughter Torah is as if he were teaching her lewdness" [*Mishnah Sotah* 3:4; *Sotah* 20a]); and preclude forever the establishment of institutions for the education of women ("Let words of Torah be burned rather than be given over to women" [*Yerushalmi Sotah* 3:4]). All of these bolstered the patriarchal order, with its power relationships between the intelligentsia and the ignorant, enslavers and enslaved, masters and servants – an order summed up briefly by R. David Abudarham (1340): "A woman is subservient to her husband, to meet his needs"[9]). The sages detailed the sorts of labor a woman was obligated to perform in order to meet her husband's needs: "These are the duties a wife must perform for her husband: grinding [flour] and baking [bread], washing clothes and cooking food, nursing her child, making his bed, and working in wool. [If she brings him servants, she may avoid some or all of these tasks, depending on the number of servants, but] Rabbi Eliezer said, 'Even if she brings him a hundred servants he should compel her to work in wool, for idleness leads to immorality'" (*Mishnah Ketubbot* 5:5). In the twelfth century, Maimonides sharply explained what that meant: "Any woman who declines to perform any of the labors that she is obligated to do is compelled to do so, even with the rod" (Maimonides, *Mishneh Torah*, *Hilkhot Ishut* 21:1). He added that "Her handiwork is her husband's… and she must serve him" (21:4). Even earlier, the Talmud anchored the relationship between the sexes in an ancient myth for the benefit of readers of Scripture who failed to pay attention to the verse "And he shall rule over you": "Was it not to Adam's gain that he was deprived of a rib and a handmaid presented to him in its stead to serve him?" (*Sanhedrin* 39b). That incisive statement is connected to the striking but infrequently noted fact that the words for "servant" "maidservant" and "family" are connected in various languages: in Hebrew, they are, respectively, *shifḥah* (specifically, a maidservant) and *mishpaḥah*; the English "family" is derived from the Latin *famulus*, servant or slave, and is

---

[9] Abudarham, *Perush ha-berakhot ve-ha-tefillot* [Commentary on the blessings and prayers], Jerusalem: 1973, 25.

related to the master's cadre of servants.[10] The rabbinic Hebrew term for sexual relations is *tashmish*, associated with a utensil that may be put to use (*lehishtamesh*) and with providing service (*leshamesh*), or *be'ilah*, an assertion of "ownership" (*ba'alut*). That is, the handmaid given to Adam to serve him – Eve, the mother of all humans and archetype of all women, who "is subservient to her husband, to meet his needs" (as Abudarham put it) – is delivered to Adam's sexual dominion and bound to do whatever task he imposes on her. He is the owner and she is the property, as the Mishnah states in the context of describing how various sorts of property are acquired: "A woman is acquired in [any of] three ways – by a document, by money, or by sexual relations" (*Kiddushin* 1:1). That a woman is her husband's property is suggested as well by Maimonides' words quoted earlier, for the human property's refusal to obey the master authorizes the master to employ force, including flogging, to compel obedience. Jewish law did not act in isolation, and various cultures expressed male-female relationships in terms of acquisition and ownership; subordination and obedience; compulsion, punishment, flogging, and taming. Roman law uses the term *sub virga* ("under the rod," indicating the master's authority to flog his subordinates to punish or train them) to convey the idea of a woman being subordinate to her husband in the same manner as a slave. The English expression "rule of thumb" in punitive context derives from the idea that the husband may flog his wife with a rod no wider than a thumb[11] – his right to discipline her by flogging was not

---

[10] Beatrice Gottlieb, *The Family in the Western World: From the Black Death to the Industrial Age* (New York: Oxford Univ. Press, 1993), 7.

[11] On the various historical, legal and mythical dimensions of the expression "rule of thumb" see: http://www.debunker.com/texts/ruleofthumb.html. The historical core of the expression in punitive context is presented as follows: "In the course of rendering rulings on cases before them, two Southern judges had alluded to an

questioned; the only issue was the maximum width of the rod he was permitted to use. The halakhic responsa literature includes discussions of husbands beating their wives, and Avraham Grossman's studies of violence against women amply document it.[12] Domestic violence today – or, more precisely, the beating by men of women and children – flows directly from this ancient notion of the husband's rights and the wife's duties, a notion that continues to exert influence even when social and legal norms have significantly changed.

The biblical world recognized a range of public roles for women; they acted as poets and prophets (Miriam, Deborah, Huldah); political leaders (Deborah, Jezebel, Athaliah, the Queen of Sheba); or sources of wisdom and sage counsel (Abigail "of good understanding" [1 Sam. 25:3], the wise woman of Tekoa, the Queen of Sheba). In rabbinic times, however, the situation changed.

In the world of the sages, these modes of socialization were closed to women and all sorts of self-realization – other than through marriage and motherhood – were precluded. The lives of women in the Jewish community came to be shaped by the position of the sages, who limited the

---

'ancient law' according to which a man could beat his wife as long as the implement was not wider than his thumb." The modern discussion on violence against women used this forgotten source somewhat inaccurately. One example is to be found in the writing of the American feminist Del Martin, who wrote in 1976: "Our law, based upon the old English common-law doctrines, explicitly permitted wife-beating for correctional purposes. However… the common-law doctrine had been modified to allow the husband 'the right to whip his wife, provided that he used a switch no bigger than his thumb' – a rule of thumb, so to speak." See the website above for the complex debate on this matter.

[12] Avraham Grossman, *Pious and Rebellious: Jewish Women in Medieval Europe*, trans. from the Hebrew by Jonathan Chipman. Waltham, MA: Brandeis Univ. Press; Hanover, NH: Univ. Press of New England, 2004, 212–230.

place of women to home and family and valued them solely as wives to their husbands and mothers to their children, barring them from participation in the circles of holiness and study. Some scholars considered the important effect on the sages' worldview of the legal reforms introduced by the Roman Emperor Augustus in the first century C.E. The reforms aimed to strengthen family life from an androcentric point of view and to encourage and enforce procreation. Other scholars, however, regard the Jewish worldview and androcentric-procreative legislation as an internal socio-cultural development related to the theological and legal disputes between the School of Hillel, which stressed procreation, and the School of Shammai, which adopted a more abstemious and ascetic position. The foregoing quotations from hallowed and influential Jewish sources represent in any event only a very small percentage of the underlying cultural and legal premises that, in extreme cases, transformed women into enslaved dolts, ruled over by husbands who were free to beat them and impose their wills on them while expecting them to be procreative, dependent, ignorant, and obedient. The discriminatory *halakhah* was uniform throughout all Jewish communities, and its rules applied regardless of geographical location ("all happy families resemble one another"). Its principles, established without exception by men – who possessed exclusive intellectual authority, inasmuch as they were holier by reason of being obligated to observe the commandments – applied equally to all subordinated women and all dominant men. But the suffering it caused took diverse forms ("every unhappy family is unhappy in its own way"), and each community had its own mechanisms for expressing the differing rights of men and women in the practical world and enforcing enslavement, discrimination, silence, and exclusion in various areas. In many communities, twelve-year-old girls were married to thirteen-year-old boys,[13] and in some communities, the engaged girls were overfed and fattened to the point of immobility in order to make them pleasing to their husbands or were kept in closed rooms until their wedding. Some communities permitted sexual relations between maidservants and members of the family,[14] and in some communities many women in their despair fled to Christian convents.[15]

Reflecting a single-mindedly masculine perspective on the role and place of women, Jewish culture developed various ways to express the patriarchal stereotypes that were used to orchestrate and justify the dominion of men over women, the prejudices of men about women, the lack of trust in women and their abilities, the sexual suspicions inevitably involved in relations between rulers and ruled, the fear of unbridled sexuality, the ambivalence of desire and attraction versus power and fear,

---

[13] See Jacob Katz, *Tradition and Crisis; Jewish Society at the End of the Middle Ages*, trans. from the Hebrew by Bernard Dov Cooperman (Harvard University Press 1993), 135–144; cf. Grossman, *Pious and Rebellious* (n. 12 above), 33–67.

[14] See Elliott Horowitz, "*Bein adonim li-mesharetot ba-ḥevrah ha-yehudit ha-eropit bein yemei ha-benayim le-reshit ha-et ha-ḥadashah*" [Between masters and maidservants in European Jewish society from the Middle Ages to early modern times] in *Eros, erusin ve-issurim: miniyut u-mishpaḥah ba-historiyah* [*Sexuality and the Family in History*], edited by Israel Bartal and Isaiah Gafni, 193–212. (Jerusalem: Merkaz Zalman Shazar, 1998).

[15] In 1730, an order of nuns, known as the Union of Maria, was organized in Lithuania to baptize Jewish girls. Between its founding and 1820, some two thousand young Jewish women were converted to Christianity under its auspices. See Meir Balaban, *Le-toledot ha-tenu`ah ha-frankit* [On the history of the Frankist movement] (Tel-Aviv, 1934), vol. 1, p. 92; Judith Kalik, *Ha-kenesiyah ha-katolit ve-ha-yehudim be-mamlekhet polin-lita ba-me'ot 17–18* [*The Catholic Church and the Jews in the Polish-Lithuanian Commonwealth in the Seventeenth and Eighteenth Centuries*] (doctoral disstertation, Hebrew Univ. 1998), 104.

and the tension between the educated class and the ignorant who depend on their grace. The adages we encounter include "A woman is solely for beauty; a woman is solely for children" (*Ketubbot* 59a); "There is no wisdom in women except at the spindle" (*Yoma* 66b); "Women's minds are frivolous" (*Shabbat* 33b); and "Gentiles, slaves, women, fools, and minors are ineligible to serve as witnesses" (*Bava Batra* 155a). The term "a woman's place" or "woman's status" reflects the question of where women are forbidden to stand. The inclusion of women in the last of foregoing maxims, along with gentiles, slaves, fools, and minors – that is, those who are not members of the community from birth and naturally are denied rights or those who suffer disabilities that prevent their participation in communal life – declares their status and indicates where they are barred from the court, the study hall, the town hall, the school, the synagogue, the yeshiva, the primary school, the advanced yeshiva, the library, and other communal institutions of learning, authority, and justice. The voices heard within those walls were exclusively male.

Those who enslave others typically try to find irrefutable justification for the enslavement, either by portraying the enslaved group in highly negative terms or by asserting divine authorization for their subjugation. The present case is no exception. It is interesting to pursue the transformation of woman from "helper and support" to "enslaved," "service provider," "rib" or "servant" who, in Maimonides' words, "may be compelled, even with the rod" or, as Sophocles's Theban king puts it, "must be constrained."

In the ancient book of Tobit, dating from the fourth or third century B.C.E. and included in the Apocrypha, the title character, in prayer on his wedding night, describes God's purpose in creating woman: "Blessed are you, O God of our ancestors, and blessed is your name in all generations forever. Let the heavens and the whole creation bless you forever. You made Adam, and for him you made his wife Eve as a helper and support. From the two of them the human race has sprung."[16] In the introduction to *Tur Even ha-Ezer*, a halakhic compendium dealing with relations between the sexes, the author (R. Jacob ben Asher, *Ba'al ha-Turim*, 1270–1343) describes the Creator's intention in gentle terms: "And he made it [the rib taken from Adam] into a woman and brought her to him as a help and to benefit him." Others, however, portray the relationship more callously: "A woman is subservient to her husband, to meet his needs" (Abudarham, *Perush ha-tefilot*, 25); "Her handiwork is her husband's... and she must serve him" (Maimonides, *Mishnch Torah*, *Hilkhot Ishut* 21:4).

How did these women who had to serve their husbands all their lives – washing their feet, making their beds, cooking their food, weaving, sewing, laundering their clothes, and running their households, all while bearing and raising their children – feel about it? A response that cuts to the quick appears in a text by a non-Jewish writer, a woman obligated to earn her own living, who examines her culture from the margins rather than from the hegemonic perspective. The writer was Charlotte Brontë (1816–1855), the author of *Jane Eyre*, who wrote this letter when she was twenty years old. I cite her because there are no texts written by Jewish women that describe their subservience:

> Following my father's advice – who from my childhood has counselled me just in the wise and friendly tone of your letter – I have endeavoured not only attentively to observe all the duties a woman ought to fulfil, but to feel deeply interested in them. I don't always succeed, for sometimes when I'm teaching or sewing I would rather be reading or writing; but I try to deny

[16] Tobit 8:5–6 (NRSV).

> myself; and my father's approbation amply rewarded me for the privation.[17]

The hostility toward women on the part of the powerful men who compel women to serve them, who "make use of" of the women "given over to their use" and their dominion, is evident in the stereotypical language that has demonized women, since antiquity, as sinners responsible for human mortality. At the beginning of the second century B.C.E., the priest Joshua Ben-Sira says, "From a woman sin had its beginning and because of her we all die" (Sirach 25:24). In his retelling of the Creation story, the author of 2 Enoch portrays God as saying, "And while he was sleeping, I took from him a rib. And I created for him a wife, so that death might come [to him] by his wife" (2 Enoch 30:17[18]). Saul of Tarsus or Paul, who was raised among the Pharisees and stressed woman's secondary status, her sin and her punishment, explains punishment for sin: "Let a woman learn in silence with full submission. I permit no woman to teach or to have authority over a man; she is to keep silent. For Adam was formed first, then Eve; and Adam was not deceived, but the woman was deceived and became a transgressor" (1 Timothy 2:11–14). Because of Eve's sin, women were forbidden to teach men; because Eve was led astray and sinned, men should teach and study in every community while women should remain silent, obedient, and uncritical. Eve's duty of obedience to Adam becomes the obligation of women in general to be silently obedient to their husbands. Women are considered to be deficient not only because

---

[17] Elizabeth Cleghorn Gaskell, *The Life of Charlotte Brontë* (1857), Chapter 8. Charlotte Brontë had written to the poet Robert Southey, asking his opinion of her poetry. The excerpt quoted above is part of her answer to his reply.

[18] Trans. from *The Old Testament Pseudepigraphia,* edited by James H. Charlesworth, vol. 1, 152. New York: Doubleday, 1983–1985.

they are secondary creatures, as suggested by the story of Adam's rib, but also because they are sinners, responsible not only for the mortality decreed against man but also for all his sexual transgressions, inasmuch as they are seen as dangerous seductresses: "When Eve was created, Satan was created with her" (*Genesis Rabbah* 7). Their inferior status as culpable sinners was justly decreed, and it implies that they require oversight, instruction, and domination: "A woman [before marriage] is a shapeless lump and concludes a covenant only with him who transforms her [into] a [useful] vessel, as it is written, 'For thy maker is thy husband; the Lord of Hosts is his name' [Isaiah 54:5]" (*Sanhedrin* 22b). These passages amply demonstrate the transformation of woman from a thinking subject to a silent object meant to satisfy the needs of its owner.

The ancient stereotypes evident in the comments attributed to Jacob's son Reuben – accused of raping or acting with cruel insolence toward his father's concubine Bilhah (Gen. 35:22; 49: 3–4) – are emblematic of the widespread blame-the-victim mentality: "For women are evil, my children, and by reason of their lacking authority or power over man, they scheme treacherously how they might entice him to themselves by means of their looks.... Women are more easily overcome by the spirit of promiscuity than are men. They contrive in their hearts against men, then by decking themselves out they lead men's minds astray."[19]

From its inception, feminism warned of the dangers inherent in regarding women as eternally marked by a demeaning, confining stereotype. It likewise cautioned against the tendency to deny women their own history – a tendency that goes back to the Genesis genealogies in which women are mentioned solely as anonymous mothers and daughters

---

[19] Testament of Reuben 5:1–3 (Charlesworth, vol. 1, 784).

while men are listed as fathers and sons bearing names that make them part of historical memory.

By denying women's history and ascribing to them an unchanging, stereotypical nature, men can more easily write mythical stories about their threatening qualities and pass general judgments that deny their humanity and make them the eternal enemy: "For women are evil, my children…." (Testament of Reuben 5:1)[20]; "I find more bitter than death the woman" (Eccl. 7:26); "When Eve was created, Satan was created with her" (*Genesis Rabbah* 7). These are striking examples of power relationships that mark, suppress, exclude, and silence a particular group by means of stereotypical generalizations while using the converse generalizations to endow another group with power, virtue, wisdom, resources, and exclusive authority. These two tendencies are evident throughout Jewish history in law and myth alike, both of them written solely from a male point of view.

An interesting series of paradoxes may be noted here. In reality, masculinity is the determinative principle of the natural order, for – as all historical sources suggest – it is men who have the power to kill or let live; nevertheless, it is women who are portrayed in myth as deadly. In reality, it is men who commit rape, yet it is women who are portrayed in myth as seductresses by their very nature – and therefore responsible for rape. In reality, men shape the normal and normative majority that is linked directly to the sacred (for only men are sanctified by the commandments and only they bear the tradition of God's Ineffable Name); women constitute the exceptional, deficient, and marginalized "other." In myth, however, women are Liliths, powerful demonic queens able to pollute men, and it is they who bear the Ineffable Name, as the Lilith myth suggests. In reality, men have exclusive control over knowledge; yet myth portrays women as

---

[20] J.H. Charlesworth. *The Old Testament Pseudepigrapha.* Garden City, NJ: 1983, 784.

sorceresses. Mastery of the magic arts (*ḥarashim*) is a quality highly valued and much needed by members of the Sanhedrin, who are exclusively male, but the same verbal root applied to women yields the derogatory Aramaic term for sorceress (*ḥarashta*), a dangerous figure. And the phenomenon is not unique to Jewish languages: both words are associated with the Greek root that refers to the blending of curative drugs and that underlies the English "pharmacy." But a man to whom the root is applied is a *pharmaceus* ("pharmacist"), while a woman is a *pharmacea* ("sorceress" or "witch")! In practice, violence is directed at women; in myth, women are associated with demonic and magical forces that symbolize evil and moral decay. It is hardly surprising that, in a culture that posits as divine law that "Thou shalt not suffer a sorceress to live" (Ex. 22:17), the Mishnah says (*Avot* chap. 2), "The more women, the more sorcery" and tells that Simeon b. Shetah hanged eighty sorceresses in Ashkelon (*Sanhedrin* 6:6). As early as the second century B.C.E., Ben-Sirach – a book marked by a strong androcentric viewpoint and one that declares "From a woman sin had its beginning, and because of her we all die" (Sirach 25:24) – sums up a father's concerns about his daughter: "A daughter is a secret anxiety to her father and worry over her robs him of sleep.... [I]t is woman who brings shame and disgrace" (Sirach 42:9–14).

Harsh was the fate of men who begot daughters in a patriarchal society that, among other things, allowed a father to sell his daughter as a maidservant and recognized the right of the paterfamilias to the sexual favors of maidservants within the household. The Talmud uses striking language to describe their fate: "Woe to one whose children are female" (*Bava Batra* 15b). The father is charged with protecting his daughter's sexuality until it is lawfully transferred to her husband in exchange for payment of the bride price that entitles the husband to take possession of her sexually and otherwise; the father's difficulties in that role are detailed in an androcentric talmudic passage that illuminates, through its endorsement of Ben Sira's depiction of matters, the hegemonic narrative that shapes the image of the subservient class:

> A daughter is a vain treasure to her father:
> Through anxiety on her account, he cannot sleep at night.
> As a minor, lest she be seduced;
> In her majority, lest she play the harlot;
> As an adult, lest she be not married;
> If she marries, lest she bear no children;
> If she grows old, lest she engage in witchcraft![21]

These poetic words embody well the argument that "gender" is the meaning that culture, by force of myth, poem, and law, ascribes to natural differences. Paraphrasing Franz Fanon ("What matters is to liberate the black man from enslavement to the archetypes of white men"[22]), one may say that what matters is to liberate women from enslavement to the archetypes of men.

It seems that from the male perspective, a woman is not a discernable, sovereign personality; she is, rather, a sort of hybrid phenomenon to be interpreted in a way that warrants dominating her. She is always suspected and threatening, seductive and deviant, enticing and corrupting – all qualities connected with the need to control her sexuality and modesty. Within the traditional world, however, no one recounts the suffering of the young person sold by her father to her husband, the pain and degradation suffered by the rape victim, the torments endured by one experiencing

---

[21] *Sanhedrin* 100b.

[22] Franz Fanon, *Peau Noire, Masques Blancs.* Translated into Hebrew by Tamar Kaplinsky. Tel Aviv: 2004, 175.

incest within the family, or the suffering and degradation of one living in a polygamous family (permitted to men in general under the Biblical and Mishnaic patriarchal order). No one in the traditional world – in which writing was the exclusive preserve of men – ever asked why the incest prohibitions listed in Leviticus do not expressly forbid sexual relations between father and daughter; no one ever described the hardships associated with annual pregnancy from very early age to menopause, perpetual nursing, and sorrowful child-rearing; and no one ever wrote about the terror of living in proximity to the unspeakable incest to be found in many families (the statistics of the Association of Rape Crisis Centers in Israel claim that 40 percent of rapes are incestuous!). Nor did anyone describe the frustration of one called upon, as "woman of the house," to devote all her time and energy to serving her husband and satisfying his every need or explain the despair of a woman absolutely dependent on her husband for her living.[23]

To the passages quoted earlier one could easily add others pertaining to the laws of levirate marriage, rape, abandoned wives unable to remarry, modesty, confinement to the home, inheritance, and slavery, as well as many other laws that denied women equality of opportunity, freedom of movement, freedom of expression, freedom from slavery, equality of resources, and equality before the law. All of them were written by men possessed of power, knowledge, freedom of speech, and authority within a society in which there existed two sorts of people: men with rights, who could easily become oppressors, and women lacking rights, who could

[23] These burdens are described to an extent, from the perspective of women in the modern world, in such works as Virginia Woolf, *A Room of One's Own* (London: Harcourt 1929;) and *Three Guineas* (London: Harcourt 1938); Adrienne Rich, *Of Woman Born* (New York: Norton 1967); and Marilyn French, *The Women's Room* (Boston: Summit 1977).

easily become oppressed. This sophisticated system of oppression, relying on the authority of religion and tradition and on the social norms common in the surrounding world, could operate because of the traditional world's fundamental recognition of two sorts of people – those "equals" of the sanctified male sex,[24] bound by the commandments and enjoying divinely ordained dominion, grounded in sacred myth; and those differing from it and subordinate to it, who, by reason of that subordination, are exempt from the commandments and therefore far less sanctified. Because of this distinction, Jewish law differed for the "equal" that is, the "worthy" – sanctified men, free to study, teach, work, earn a living, and rule over their wives, and for the "different" – non-sanctified women, subject to the yoke of household, family, and ruler-husband and relegated to silence and obedience. The law provided for different sets of rights, based on the gender of the group's members and the number of commandments by which they were bound.

Various societies in the non-Jewish world developed the distinction between men and women in accord with the ideas of Aristotle, who provided a basis for the widespread view that women were naturally inferior and men naturally superior. Aristotle drew a substantive distinction between the two sexes, identifying men with form and spirit and women with physicality and matter. The spiritual virtues of men entitled them to rule; the negative qualities of women dictated that they be ruled. This distinction between spirit and matter, between soul and body, implies as

---

[24] See Maimonides's explanation of why a man has priority over a woman with respect to being kept alive: "You already know that all the commandments are binding on males, but females are bound only by some of them, as explained in Tractate *Kiddushin*. He is therefore more sanctified than she, and that is why a man has priority in being kept alive" (Maimonides, *Commentary on the Mishnah*, *Horayot* 3:7).

well the distinction between active and passive, between rational and non-rational, between possessor and possessed (sexually and otherwise), and between ruler and ruled. It is no wonder that the Aristotelian rule reserved spirituality to men and that the English word "virtue" derives from the Latin for "man" (*vir*; cf. also "virile"). Conversely, materiality became the domain of women, as evidenced by the relationship of the Latin word for mother (*mater*) to matter, which Aristotle held inferior to spirit.

The role assigned to women in traditional society was exclusively to act as mother and wife, serving her husband and satisfying his needs and serving the members of the household. A woman's sexuality, ruled over by her husband and expressed solely within marriage and motherhood, was regarded as the essence of her being. The community afforded no recognition to a woman's rights over her body and spirit outside the patriarchal family or to her right to acquire an education, pursue a trade, or participate in communal life. It even declined to recognize her freedom of expression or of movement or her right to choose a spouse or to decide to remain single and not bear children. (Biblical Hebrew lacks any word for "bachelor," either male or female.) A fortiori, it did not recognize her right to live with a female partner or to devote her life to some purpose other than service of husband and family.

In light of these gloomy circumstances, it comes as no surprise that the literary oeuvre of the People of the Book over many centuries – from the song of biblical Deborah (Judges 5) to the stories of Devorah Baron (1887–1956) – includes no widely-known Hebrew-language works written by women.[25] This literary silence within a learned community, a community that expected all its sons to be literate but until recently denied all its daughters the opportunity to take part in learning, means that its entire

---

[25] See Elior, "'*Nokheḥot nifkadot*'" (above, n. 5).

written output – law, literature, myth, mysticism, poetry, and culture – was produced exclusively by men. This exclusively masculine conception and representation of the world affords no voice to the viewpoint of girls, young women, engaged women, wives, mothers, widows, divorcees, servants and mistresses, matriarchs, victims of rape and incest, captive women, female victims of violence, ignorant and subjugated women, lunatics and women possessed by a dybbuk. The life experiences of women – their feelings, values, desires, frustrations, and suffering and their wisdom, insights, and perspectives – form no part of the written discourse, the interpretive tradition, or the cultural heritage. Life-sustaining feminine values such as compassion, nurturing, fellowship, cooperation, and opposition to war and coercion seem to be situated at the bottom of the masculine hierarchy of values, just as women's illnesses are disparagingly labeled. It is enough in that regard to recall that hysteria, seen in the masculine medical literature as a typically feminine affliction, is related to *hystera*, Greek for "uterus."[26] The moon, or *luna*, a feminine symbol since antiquity because its monthly cycle seemed to resemble that of women, is linked in many languages to words for madness; in English, the pertinent term is "lunacy."

As far as I know, there exists no Jewish text written within the traditional world in Hebrew or Aramaic that conveys a woman's perspective on her father, her husband, or her children or on the oppressive traditional structure in which they lived. From the "book of the generations of Adam" (Gen. 5), which names all the male progenitors of humanity but

---

[26] See Ron Barkai, "*Masorot refu'iyot yevaniyot ve-hashpa`atan al tefisat ha-ishah bi-yemei ha-beinayyim*" (Greek medical traditions and their influence on the understanding of women in the Middle Ages). In Yael Azmon, ed., *Eshnav le-ḥayyehen shel nashim be-ḥevrot yehudiyot* (*A View into the Lives of Women in Jewish Societies.* Jerusalem): Merkaz Zalman Shazar, 1995, 127–128.

passes in silence over the females, to the histories of Jewish communities, which refer only to men, women have simply been erased from memory. Zionism inherited many of these modes of oppression, discrimination, and obliviousness, as is readily evident in the diaries of women who immigrated to and worked in the Land of Israel in the early days of the Zionist movement and in the texts gathered during the second half of the twentieth century by Rahel Katznelson-Shazar, Bracha Habas, Michal Hagati, Yaffa Berlovitz, Margalit Shiloh, and Tamar Hess. At the same time, however, Hebrew literature opened unexpected doors to examination of women's lives in past generations, from the closing lines of Bialik's well-known poem "*Shiv`ah*" (Seven days of mourning)[27] and to Agnon's story "*Bi-demi yamehah*" ("In the Midst of Her Days"), whose famous opening sentence offers a penetrating sketch of the lot his mother shared with countless other women: "In the midst of her days my mother died, at the age of about thirty-one. Few and hard were the years of her life. All day she sat at home, not leaving the house."[28] Author Ḥayyim Be'er's mother and grandmother – the latter raised in the Ḥaredi world and unable even to read – who are artistically portrayed in his *Ḥavalim*, and the very well-read but tormented mother of Amos Oz, described in his *Tale of Love and Darkness*, afford the reader a glimpse into the world of women who were unable to tell their own stories but whose sons afforded them incomparable voices. Poet and essayist Joseph Brodsky offers a heartwarming account of his mother's harsh life in Soviet Russia in his essay "In a Room and a Half" (in *Less Than One: Selected Essays*)[29]; it, too, provides a wonderful peek at a world that has disappeared. In his book of essays entitled

---

[27] In H.N. Bialik, *Poems*. Tel Aviv: 1935, 199.

[28] In *Kol kitvei Shmuel Yosef Agnon* (The collected writings of S.Y. Agnon). 1975, vol. 5.

[29] New York: Farrar, Straus & Giroux, 1985

Reshimot al makom, Ariel Hirschfeld portrays his mother and his relative, Savta Shoshanah, thereby opening a window on a largely unknown world of women living painful lives. These accounts are of tremendous importance, for until the twentieth century, the Jewish community lacked any documents examining society from a feminine point of view or presenting any critical, alternative stance vis-à-vis that society. To this day, there is almost no historical or literary documentation of mothers written by women.

During the last third of the seventeenth century, we hear of the first challenge to the patriarchal order, voiced by a highly unusual man, the kabbalist Shabbetai Zevi (1626–1676), who saw himself as a redeemer able to transcend limits and change the world order. Among his followers, Shabbetai Zevi was understood to be a woman, as is evident from the words of Jacob Frank, one of those who carried on his legacy: "It was said of the former (Shabbetai Zevi) that he was secretly of the female sex."[30] Shabbetai Zevi, who considered himself and was considered by others to be androgynous,[31] was unique in his identification with women and their suffering. His several marriages ended in divorce because of his inability to live up to what was expected of a husband, but he remained very friendly with his former wives throughout his life and partook of their society, contrary to the pertinent halakhic prohibitions. Men and women in Sabbatean groups rewarded him, during the eighteenth century, with songs

[30] See Rachel Elior, "*Sefer divrei ha-adon le-Ya`akov Frank*" (Jacob Frank's "*Divrei ha-adon*"), in *Ha-ḥalom ve-shivro: ha-tenu`ah ha-shabta'it u-sheluḥotehah – meshiḥiyut, shabta'ut, u-frankizm* (*The Sabbatean Movement and Its Aftermath: Messianism, Sabbateanism and Frankism* Edited by Rachel Elior, vol. 2, 534. Jerusalem: 2001.

[31] See *Sefer shirot ve-tishbaḥot shel ha-shabta'im* (The Sabbatean book of hymns and praises), trans. Moshe Atiash, annotated by Gershom Scholem, introduction by Yizhak Ben-Zvi. Tel Aviv: 1948), 37, 64, 156, 211.

of praise written in Donmeh circles (Sabbateans who acted outwardly as converts to Islam but continued to practice certain Jewish rituals): "Shabbetai Zevi, the *Shekhinah*, liberated us."[32] The Protestant clergyman Thomas Coenen, who served as minister of the Dutch Reformed Church in Izmir during the last third of the seventeenth century, provides an instructive account of Shabbetai Zevi's biting critique of the position of women in the Jewish community. Widely regarded by scholars of the period as a reliable witness, Coenen recounts Shabbetai Zevi's actions in his town:

> He tried to attract the friendship of women and to make himself pleasing to them.... When he was in their company, he would quote verse 10 of Ps. 45: "Kings' daughters are among your favorites; at your right hand stands the queen in gold of Ophir." He would then add his own words: "You pitiful women, how unfortunate you are; for on Eve's account you suffer such great pains when you give birth. Even worse, you are enslaved to your husbands, and you cannot do anything, small or great, without their agreement; and so forth. But give thanks to God that I have come into the world to redeem you from all your torments and to liberate you and make you as happy as your husbands; for I have come to annul the sin of primeval Adam."[33]

---

[32] Id., 99.

[33] Thomas Coenen, *Ydele verwachtinge der Joden getoont in den Persoon van Sabethai Zevi* (*Vain Hopes of the Jews as Revealed in the Figure of Sabbetai Zevi*). Trans. into Hebrew from the Dutch by Asher Artur Lagavir and Efrayim Shemu'eli, introduction and notes by Yosef Ḳaplan (Jerusalem: Hotsa'at Merkaz Dinur, 1998), 54–55. (The quoted passage is translated into English from the Hebrew translation.)

Starting in the late nineteenth century and throughout the twentieth, ever since women in various communities began to enjoy the benefits of the Enlightenment and to protest vocally against the exclusivity of the male hegemonic narrative, previously silenced voices began to be heard from various directions. Credit for the first challenge by a woman to the corrupt male world of oppressors and oppressed goes to a Russian-born writer, Devorah Baron (1887–1956). The daughter of the town Rabbi of Uzda in the Minsk district, Baron wrote wonderful stories, included in her book *Parshiyot mukdamot* [Early episodes], about her father's court. In them, she gives voice to the cries of Ashkenazi Jewish women who suffered their husbands' cruelty and violence, imposed under the cover of privacy. Bracha Serri (b. 1940), a writer and poet of Yemenite origin, publicized the cruel meaning of the seeming "good" concealed behind the doors of the traditional Yemenite household. In her terrifying story "*Keri`ah*" (Tearing) (1983), she unmasks the horror lurking behind the intimacy of personal matters and embodies the feminist slogan that "the personal is political." The story cries out with the torment suffered by Yemenite women sold by avaricious fathers into arranged marriages with wealthy men and subjected to sexual relations with husbands acting, in effect, as wedding-night rapists hastening to engage in religiously obligatory sexual relations even though their brides were children ignorant of sexuality.[34] In *Mi-mizraḥ shemesh*

[34] Beracha Serri (*Pu`ah Meri-Dor*). "Keri`ah." In *Nogah* 1 (1980); reprinted in *Ha-kol ha-aḥer* (The other voice), edited by Lili Rattok, Tel Aviv: 1994. After the story was dramatized and staged, Yemenite men mounted demonstrations against the production. Yemenite women sided with the author, however, maintaining the story accurately represented reality and that the play "was nothing in comparison to the personal suffering of many women." See Hannah Safran, *Lo roẓot liheyot neḥmadot: ha-ma'avak al zekhut ha-beḥirah le-nashim ve-reshitah shel ha-feminizm ha-ḥadash be-yisra'el* (*Don't wanna be nice girls*) (Haifa: Pardes, 2006), 127–128.

[From sunrise], the essayist Jacqueline Kahanov, an acute observer, portrays the lives of Levantine women in both the secular and traditional world in Egypt, Europe, and Israel from an unconventional perspective; and the stories of Dan Benayah Seri about women in the Bukharian community (*Ugiyyot ha-melaḥ shel savta sultana*) (Grandma Sultana's salt cakes, 1981) and *Ẓipporei ha-ẓel* (Birds of the shadow) tell of the suffering of women in the oriental Jewish communities. Writers such as Shoshanah Shebabo and Rebecca Alper provide a feminine perspective on the lives of women during the first half of the twentieth century, and there are no doubt many others who wrote about their own life experiences as well as the inadequately-known lives of earlier generations.

The work of Vered Madar on the elegies of Yemenite women casts light on fascinating dimensions of the elegists' self-consciousness (*Pe`amim* 2006), and Michal Held's doctoral dissertation on women's Ladino folk tales uncovers data related to the incestuous relations in whose shadow women lived, transforming the hegemonic story, in which the dominant player (the male) corrupts the dominated female, into the story of the dominated player, disclosing the full horror of the oppressive hegemony. The images of women in various communities depicted by Amalia Kahana Karmon – who, in her books *Bi-kefifah aḥat* (Together) and *Ve-yareaḥ be-emek ayalon* (Moon in the Valley of Ayalon) uses the power of art to preserve memory – uncover the hidden truth about family life in Israel from an unconventionally courageous feminine viewpoint. The poems of Vicki Shiran (*Shoveret kir* [Wall-breaker] 2005) and her articles in various forums point to the complex discrimination – class, economic, political, and gender-based – against oriental women in Israeli society and opened new vistas on the study of gender relationships in an immigrant society.

I have here sketched, in preliminary terms, an approach to a complex, multi-faceted problem involving battles over discrimination and exclusion, memory and its suppression. Let me conclude with seven troublesome questions that pertain to all Jewish communities and that are directed toward safeguarding the past – whether or not confined within geographical, historical, phenomenological or class bounds – from a decline into the slough of forgetfulness:

1. Did men prevent women from learning to read and write because they were concerned, consciously or unconsciously, that women's distinctive, gender-based viewpoints would shatter cultural conventions, expose the mechanisms for suppressing women, compromise the solidarity of the collective dedicated to service of God, and undermine the myth of brotherhood within the traditional, male community?
2. Did Jewish men deny Jewish women access to the centers of knowledge and authority in the public arena, consigning them to ignorance and to dependence on fathers and husbands, because of some concern about shifting the balance of power between oppressors and oppressed? Is that position related to the policy in the antebellum American South – a policy that vividly illustrates the link between enlightenment and freedom – of forbidding slaveholders, on pain of lashes, fines, and imprisonment, to teach their slaves to read and write?[35]
3. Were men, most of whom were literate, aware of how women, denied the opportunity to read and write, expressed their opposition to the

[35] Kim Warren, "Literacy and Liberation." *Reviews in American History* 33/4 (December 2005): 510–517. These laws were significantly strengthened in the wake of Nat Turner's Rebellion in 1831.

system and sought to subvert it by means of orally transmitted poetry and folktales?

4. Has the time come to stop justifying discrimination within Jewish society, as many attempt to do, on the historical grounds that surrounding societies were discriminatory as well – an attempted justification that disregards the conscious efforts of Jews to distinguish themselves from the surrounding cultures in all other respects?
5. Has the time come to examine the ways in which the traditional society's models of discrimination and exclusion, grounded in sacred texts and their norm-determining interpretations, have penetrated to the heart of the secular Zionist culture that does not recognize the sanctity of *halakhah* or "Torah opinion"?
6. Is it time for a systematic review of all laws written and interpreted by men with respect to women and to declare invalid every law reflecting androcentrism, exclusivity, discrimination, inequality, monopoly over economic resources, and sexual coercion? Are social justice, economic equality, and extirpation of patriarchy a pipe dream or a reasonable goal likely to be achieved?
7. Is the State of Israel's continued lack of an egalitarian constitution, equally applicable to all citizens, male and female alike, connected to the fact that the *Ḥaredi* parties, which neither admit women as members nor allow for their election to the Knesset, have refused to allow the word "equality" to appear in the Basic Laws, in light of everything discussed above?

Speaking Voices; Silencing Worlds; Silenced Voices

The Hebrew language has no present tense of the sort that exists in other languages. Hebrew time is either past or future, and so, too, the Jewish people: it has a great yesterday and a great tomorrow but no present whatsoever.

Ḥayyim Naḥman Bialik[1]

Does anyone seriously believe that myth and literary fiction do not refer to the real world, tell truths about it, and provide useful knowledge of it?

Hayden White[2]

---

[1] From remarks by Ḥayyim Naḥman Bialik to the Jewish-National Conference in Kiev in 1918. See Shlomo Shva, *Ḥozeh lekh beraḥ: sippur hayyav shel ḥayyim Naḥman Bialik* [*O Seer, Go, Flee Away* (biography of Ḥayyim Naḥman Bialik)]. (Tel Aviv: Devir , 1990), 175.

[2] "'Figuring the Nature of the Times Deceased': Literary Theory and Historical Writing." In *The Future of Literary Theory*, edited by Ralph Cohen, 39. New York and London: Rutledge, 1989.

Introduction

The modern consciousness associates modern times with progress, science, humanism, enlightenment, human autonomy, individual free choice, rational thought and critical inquiry – all based on a growing separation between natural and supernatural categories, between rationality and irrationality, and between the tangible and the concealed. The written record, however, is not so straightforward. Intricately reflecting the intellectual world, the spiritual consciousness and the social reality at the beginning of the modern era, it offers an endlessly complex view of the world, revealing the substantial weight assigned to irrational elements within the socio-cultural environment. That record allows us to see clearly that the supernatural world, which connects celestial beings with the human realm, and the abnormal world, which connects deceased souls to living bodies, constituted an important dimension within the period's social reality and religious and cultural tapestry – a dimension in which the physical was interwoven with the metaphysical and the concepts of the invisible world were used to interpret the visible world.

Jewish religious creativity in early modern times developed in a universe containing no empty space. It was a world in which concealed and revealed realities were interwoven in a complex network of invisible forces and mythic beings, *hekhalot* (heavenly sanctuaries) and *sefirot* (divine emanations), souls and spirits, angels and demons, visions and dreams. That network, which connected the human world to representations of the sacred world and eternal life through a system of concepts termed *yiḥud* (union) and *devekut* (bonding), connected the human world to the world of impurity and death through a system of concepts termed *gilgul* (transmigration of souls) and dybbuk (an "attachment"; the term is a short form derived from a seventeenth-century Yiddish folk usage, "an attachment [dybbuk] from the outside forces," that is, the evil spirits[3]). This religious oeuvre stood at the high-water mark of dualistic kabbalistic thought, which forged a new conceptual language for the experience of exile and the yearning for redemption, connecting concrete historical experience with the supernatural world and the hidden realms. Kabbalah interpreted human activity within the context of the polarity between forces of good and of evil, holiness and impurity, the *Shekhinah* (God's presence) and the husk (*kelipah*, a representation of evil), the eternal world and the world of death. It instilled new meaning into humanity's relationships with these realms, linked on the one hand to the anticipated redemption and the realm of sacred forces and purity and, on the other, to the exile and the realm of impurity and evil forces, into which the nation was now cast.

In large part, these developments were the work of kabbalists of the generation of the expulsion from Spain, active in the late fifteenth and early sixteenth centuries. The exiles and their children, who arrived in the Ottoman Empire of the 1520s, were the kabbalists of the mid-1530s to the mid-1580s who immigrated to Safed, led by their messianic expectations, pietistic world-view and mystical inspiration. Safed, the ingathering of Jewish immigrants from conflicting cultures – the Moslem East and the Christian West – was the center of considerable social tensions and mystical arousal that generated pietistic and ascetic values, as well as diversified spiritual ideas and new interest in the mysterious and magical realms. The pious and ascetic teachers and disciples, who were endowed with mystical inspiration, exerted an influence both on intellectual discourse within learned circles – which reflected on the hidden meaning of exile and redemption, on wandering souls and bodies, on exiled divinity and human redemption – and on popular thought inspired by the kabbalistic

---

[3] See Gershom Scholem, "Dibbuk." In *Encyclopedia Judaica* (Jerusalem: 1971), vol. 1, cols. 19–21.

theory of the soul and its life before and after death. These mystical ideas that were anchored in the hermeneutical study of the *Zohar* (Book of Splendor) achieved broad dissemination through kabbalistic morality literature and its popular versions as adapted in conduct literature, hagiography, pietistic literature and folk tales.

Within this literature, concrete human activities mandated by the tradition – such as observance of the commandments, prayer, Torah study, laws, and customs – were linked to internalized spiritual concepts tied to the realm of holiness. The latter include *kavvanot* (intentions while performing commandments or praying); *yiḥudim* ("unions"; recitations to promote God's union with the *Shekhinah*); *tikkun* (repairing rifts in the cosmic fabric, intending thereby to hasten redemption); raising the sparks (the shards of holiness scattered, according to kabbalistic myth, when the primeval sacred vessels were broken, a cosmic catastrophic event reflected in the continuous state of exile on earth); *devekut*, (attachment, cleaving, bonding, union and communion with God – all intended to promote redemption through intellectual, contemplative and emotional concentration on the divine realm); *mesirut nefesh* (dedication, even to the point of giving one's life); *berurim* (purifications of various dimensions of exile reflected in the subjugation to evil forces of the world of the husks); and *zivvugim* (couplings, symbolizing union of the separated worlds and redemption in heaven). These concepts were valued for their influence, according to kabbalistic myth, on the redemption of the *Shekhinah* and the subjugation of the husk. Meanwhile, sins and transgressions were interpreted as strengthening the forces of evil and the dominion of the husk – that is, the world of impurity, pictured as a photographic negative of the world of holiness. The life of the human soul is connected to hidden worlds portrayed in connection to the world of the *sefirot* and to the Garden of Eden, the treasure of the souls, *olam ha-dibbur* (the world of speech), transmigration, *ibbur* (lit., impregnation), the store-house of souls, and *kaf ha-kela* (the catapult of souls). It is thereby removed from the bounds of bodily life, of physical birth and death. The life of the soul was transformed into part of a complex system of reward and punishment that broke through the bounds of the terrestrial world and became tied to the supernatural world, extending between the poles of holiness and impurity, *Shekhinah* and husk, divinity and *sitra aḥra* ("the other side," a term for the forces of evil), redemption and exile, angels and demons, the pure world of eternal life and the impure world of the dead. The kabbalistic oeuvre raised the possibility of passageways between the revealed world and the hidden, intertwined through their connection to transmigration and dybbuk, spirits, fiends, demons, *maggidim* (heavenly voices emanating from a holy person's throat) and angels. A person could be caught up in these passageways against his or her will, entirely passively – either by positive hidden forces tied to the *Shekhinah* and the holy world of angels and *maggidim* or by negative forces tied to the *sitra aḥra*, the world of demons, and the forces of impurity.

In the early modern period, with the advent of printing and the publication (beginning in the sixteenth century) of the *Zohar* and other kabbalistic literature, this kabbalistic consciousness spread among wide circles of Jews. It became part of the interrelationship between human activity and its influence on reality, at one pole of which was the revelation of divine presence – the *sitra de-kedushah* ("holy side"), the exalted *Shekhinah*, and the hope for redemption – while, at the other pole, were the revelations of the satanic presence, the impure side, the *sitra aḥra*, the world of the husk and the yoke of exile.

A rich and variegated kabbalistic literature, written between the thirteenth and sixteenth centuries and printed at the beginning of the modern era and since, reflects the bi-polarity that influenced the concept of the divinity, the worship of God, scriptural exegesis, and the theory of the soul. In its various incarnations – in writings, discourses, printed texts, kabbalistic-ethical literature, public ceremonies, hagiography and folk tales – it affected the spiritual identity and cultural consciousness of the community as a whole. It did so through the new language of mystical concepts that it developed, a language that tied the theory of the divine to the theory of the soul within a bi-polar context and portrayed the interrelationship between the revealed and the concealed worlds and the powerful battles that took place within them between the *sitra aḥra* and the *sitra de-kedushah*.[4]

---

[4] This period in Jewish history and the conceptual world that developed within it have been the subject of numerous studies. See Gershom Scholem, *Major Trends in Jewish Mysticism.* New York: Schocken Books, 1941, 244–284; Zalman Shazar, "*Ẓofayikh Ẓefat"* [The seers of Safed]. In *Orei dorot* [Light of bygone generations]. Jerusalem: 1971, 11–30; Isaiah Tishby, *Torat ha-ra ve-ha-kelippah be-kabbalat ha-ari* (The theory of evil and the husk in Lurianic Kabbalah). Jerusalem: Akademon, 1965; Schocken Press, 1942; R. J. Zwi Werblowsky, *Joseph Karo: Lawyer and Mystic.* Oxford: Oxford University Press, 1962, 84–168; Me'ir Benayahu, ed. *Sefer toledot ha-ari: gilgul nusḥe'otav ve-erko mi-beḥinah historit* (The life of R. Isaac Luria: textual history and historical value). Jerusalem: Makhon Ben-Zvi, 1967; Rachel Elior, "Messianic Expectations and Spiritualization of Religious Life in the Sixteenth Century." *Revue d'Études Juives* 145/1–2 (1986): 35–49; id. "*Ha-ma'avak al ma'amadah shel ha-kabbalah ba-me'ah ha–16*" (The sixteenth-century battle over the place of the Kabbalah). In *Meḥkarei yerushalayim be-maḥshevet yisra'el* (*Jerusalem Studies in Jewish Thought*) 1 (1981–1982): 177–190; id., "*Ha-zikah ha-metaforit bein ha-el la-adam u-reẓifutah shel ha-mamashut ha-ḥezyonit be-kabbalat ha-ari*" (The metaphorical connection between God and man and the continuity of envisioned reality in Lurianic Kabbalah). In Rachel Elior and Judah Liebes, eds., *Kabbalat ha-ari: divrei ha-kenes ha-benle'umi ha-revi'i le-ḥeker toledot ha-mistikah ha-yehudit* [Lurianic Kabbalah: Proceedings of the Fourth Annual International Conference on the History of Jewish Mysticism] (*Meḥkarei yerushalayim be-maḥshevet yisra'el* [Jerusalem Studies in Jewish Thought] 10

In the following inquiry, I want to examine the interrelationship between, on the one hand, the conceptual world that bridges the revealed and concealed dimensions of kabbalistic reality and, on the other, popular culture and social reality within the Jewish community. I propose to do so by considering the meaning of one concept within the rich world of kabbalistic ideas that developed at the start of the modern era – the concept of the "dybbuk," defined in Jewish tradition as a deceased person's spirit

---

(Jerusalem: 1992), 47–57; R. Elior, "Exile and Redemption in Jewish Mystical Thought." *Studies in Spirituality* 14 (2004): 1–15; Michal Kushnir-Oron, "Ḥalom, ḥazon u-meẓi'ut be-sefer ha-ḥezyonot le-rabbi ḥayyim vital" [Dream, vision, and reality in R. Ḥayyim Vital's Book of Visions]. In *Kabbalat ha-ari*, ed. Elior and Liebes, supra; Yosef Ḥayyot (Jeffrey Chajes), "*Mistika'iyot yehudiyot be-aspaklariyah shel sefer ha-ḥezyonot le-rabbi ḥayyim vital*" (Female Jewish mystics in light of R. Ḥayyim Vital's Book of Visions). *Zion* 67 (2002): 139–162; Bracha Zack, *Bi-sha`arei ha-kabbalah shel rabbi mosheh kordovero* (Kabbalah of Rabbi Moshe Cordovero). Beersheba: Ben-Gurion University of the Negev Press, 1995; Gershom Scholem, *Sabbatai Sevi; The Mystical Messiah*, 1626–1676, trans. from the Hebrew by R.J. Zwi Werblowsky. Princeton: Princeton Univ. Press, 1973, 1–102; *Rabbi mosheh ḥayyim luẓatto u-venei doro: osef iggerot u-te`udot* (R. Moshe Ḥayyim Luzzatto and his contemporaries: anthology of letters and documents), introduction and annotations by Simon Ginsburg. Tel Aviv: Mossad Bialik – Devir, 1937; Me'ir Balaban, *Le-toledot ha-tenu`ah ha-frankit* (On the history of the Frankist movement), 1. Tel Aviv: Devir, 1934, 1–100; Abraham Jacob Brawer, *Galiẓiyah vi-yehudehah: meḥqarim be-toledot galiẓiyah vi-yehudehah ba-mei'ah ha-shemoneh esreh* (Galicia and its Jews: studies in the history of Galician Jewry in the eighteenth century). Jerusalem: Mossad Bialik, 1965, 197–267; Lawrence Fine, *Safed Spirituality, Rules of Mystical Piety.* New York: Paulist Press, 1984; Lewis Jacobs, "The Doctrine of the Divine Sparks," in *Studies in Rationalism, Judaism, and Universalism,* edited by Raphael Loewe. London: Routledge and Kegan Paul, 1966; Solomon Schechter, "Safed in the Sixteenth Century," in id., *Studies in Judaism* (second series). Philadelphia: Jewish Publication Society of America, 1908.

that enters a living person, detaching that person from his routine life within the bounds of accepted norms. The concept originates in the kabbalistic theory of the soul and the mystical literature pertaining to sanctity, to the husk, and to the passageways between the world of the living and the world of the dead. It made its way through various channels outside the kabbalistic texts, in contexts related to transmigration and to reprisal for sins and in connection with the theory of retribution and the kabbalistic doctrine of the soul. It became a crucial concept in interpreting the life of the body and the soul with regard to the relations between strength and weakness, illness and deviance.

The Societal Background for the Phenomenon of the Dybbuk in the Traditional World of the Sixteenth to Eighteenth Centuries

The traditional Jewish world of the late Middle Ages and early modern era was a class-based society grounded in a firm patriarchal order and strict social stratification. Within that world, the selection of a spouse was seen not as an autonomous personal decision but as a decision reached by parents acting on behalf of their young, inexperienced children who had not yet attained mature judgment. In an analysis of communal regulations, halakhic literature on the establishment of families, and biographical accounts from the Ashkenazi world during that period, historian Jacob Katz found that Jewish society acted in accord with a religious ideal that demanded early marriage. Inspired by a system of religious-cultural-moral values and adhering to socio-economic understanding grounded in a rational, utilitarian assessment, the members of the community aspired to marry off their children at the earliest possible age. The new family was established in accord with the agreement reached by the parents, the natural agents of the couple; if the parents were not living, the agreement was arranged between relatives or guardians acting as agents of the community. Weighty economic, social, and religious interests required arranged marriages, based on a series of rational considerations within the parents' discretion. The hope was that girls would be married before they reached the age of sixteen; for boys, the desirable age was no older than eighteen. Those who arranged matches at earlier ages, marrying off thirteen- and fourteen-year-old girls and fifteen- or sixteen-year-old boys were considered praiseworthy, and contemporary accounts show that marriage at the age of eleven or twelve was not uncommon. Such factors as personal compatibility or choice based on intimacy or romance were not taken into account at all and were not considered pertinent to the marriage bond. Moreover, the couple's right to choose, on the basis of chance meeting or romance, was not recognized. If a secret marriage took place without prior arrangement, it was annulled as a promiscuous denial of the authority of the parents or their agents.[5]

---

[5] Jacob Katz, "*Nisu'im ve-ḥayyei ishut be-moẓe'ei yemei ha-beinayim*" [Marriage and family life at the waning of the Middle Ages], *Zion* 10 (1954), 21–54. For an overview, see id., *Tradition and Crisis; Jewish Society at the End of the Middle Ages*, trans. from the Hebrew by Bernard Dov Cooperman. New York: New York University Press, 1993, 135–144; Israel Halpern, "*Nesu'ei behalah be-mizraḥ eropah*" (Elopements in Eastern Europe). In *Yehudim ve-yahadut be-mizraḥ eropah: meḥkarim be-toledotehem* (Jews and Judaism in Eastern Europe: studies in their history). Jerusalem: Magnes Press, 1969, 289–309. See also David Biale, *Eros and the Jews: From Biblical Israel to Contemporary America* New York: Basic Books, 1992, 64–65, 127–128. Cf. David C. Kraemer, ed., *The Jewish Family: Metaphor and Memory*. New York: Dover Publications, 1989; Jacob Goldberg, "*Al ha-nisu'in shel yehudei polin ba-me'ah ha–18*" (Marriage among eighteenth-century Polish Jews). In *Ha-ḥevrah ha-yehudit be-mamlekhet polin-lita* (*Jewish Society in the Polish Commonwealth*), translated from Polish to Hebrew by Tzofiyah Lasman. Jerusalem: Merkaz Zalman Shazar, 1999, 171–216; Israel Bartal

Having invested great effort in organizing marriage on the basis of rational considerations and societal interests, Jewish society developed a

---

and Isaiah Gafni, eds., *Eros, erusin ve-issurim: miniyut u-mishpaḥah ba-historiyah* (*Sexuality and the Family in History*). Jerusalem: Merkaz Zalman Shazar, 1998. The ages at which children were considered marriageable are reflected in the opening lines of the autobiographical account of Salomon Maimon (1753–1800): "In the fourteenth year of my life, my eldest son David was born to me. At my marriage I was only eleven years old." See *Salomon Maimon: an Autobiography*, edited and with an introduction by Moses Hadas, based on the 1888 translation from the German by J. Clark Murray. New York: Schocken Books, 1967, 33. Glikl of Hameln wrote in her memoirs, which were written between 1691 and 1719, about the early ages of the marriages that she had arranged for her children. See: *Glikl Memoirs 1691–1719,* edited and translated from the Yiddish by Chava Turniansky. Jerusalem: The Zalman Shazar Center for Jewish History, 2006, 121; Zippor, her daughter, was married at thirteen or fourteen years of age (266–268); her daughter Freidchen was twelve years old when marriage was considered (471). Dov Ber Birkental was married at the age of twelve, as appears in his journal: *Zikhronot rabbi dov mi-boleḥov* (5483–5565) (Memoirs of R. Dov of Bolechow [1723–1805]), edited by Mark Wischnitzer. Berlin: Kelal, 1922, 45. R. Naḥman of Bratslav, born in 1772, was married at the age of thirteen. See Arthur Green, *Tormented Master: A Life of Rabbi Naḥman of Bratslav.* University: Univ. of Alabama Press, 1978, 33, 283. Enlightenment literature depicted the difficulties faced by these young men who were married while they were still children. See Yisra'el Bartal, "*'Onut' ve-'ein onut' – bein masorah le-haskalah*" ["Potency" and "impotence": Between tradition and enlightenment], in Bartal and Gafni, *Eros, erusin ve-issurim*, supra, 230–234. For an assessment of women's expectations and reactions to their fulfillment from a gender-based perspective, see Adah Rapoport-Albert, "On Women in Hasidism, S.A. Horodecky and the Maid of Ludmir Tradition." *Jewish History: Essays in Honour of Chimen Abramsky*, London 1988, 495–525. In his story "Tehillah," which is based on historical fact, S.Y. Agnon notes that Tehillah was betrothed in the age of eleven and marriage planned at the age of twelve. *Kol sippurav shel Shemu'el Yosef Agnon*, 7: *Ad henah* (The collected stories of S.Y. Agnon, vol. 7). Jerusalem and Tel Aviv: Schocken, 1978, 198.

notion that providential factors were at play in matchmaking and came to regard all aspects of selecting a partner and preserving the marital bond as predestined.[6] Dissolving a marriage was no simple matter, for the union was anchored in a sacred religious tradition and dependent on complex, patriarchal, socio-economic arrangements. The religious tradition pertaining to marriage included such concepts as matches made in heaven, the marriage bond, the wedding canopy, covenant, bridal virginity, and the biblical commandment to be fruitful and multiply; the socio-economic aspects included arranging a match and setting its terms; the marriage contract, setting forth the economic obligations of the husband (or his estate) in the event of divorce or death; dowry; "acquisition" of the bride; genealogy and lineage; family; and parental support of the young couple. Divorce, accordingly, was precluded except for the weightiest of reasons, and it posed great difficulties for both spouses: it imposed a heavy economic burden on the husband, and it seriously impaired the social standing of the wife. Marriage at a young age, arranged by the parents or family agents, was the course of action favored by society. Spinsterhood by choice was entirely unknown within Jewish society, though spinsterhood compelled by various circumstances was a part of social reality – as was the occasional compelled marriage. These oppressive norms subjected young people of both sexes to great hardships. But while young men could leave their parents' homes to study Torah and might be able to find

---

[6] See Pinḥas Katzenellenbogen, *Yesh manḥilin*, edited by Yitzhak Dov Feld. Jerusalem: Makhon Ḥatam Sofer, 1986. In that eighteenth-century autobiographical account, Katzenellenbogen (b. 1691), the rabbi of Boskovitz, Moravia, tells of his matches and marriages (235–258). Cf. *Sefer Ḥasidim,* edited by Reuben Margaliot. Jerusalem: Mosad Harav Kook, 1973, sections 382–388. On the standing of women in the Middle Ages regarding marriage and divorce, see Avraham Grossman, *Pious and Rebellious,* 37–67 (marriage), 232–252 (divorce); see also Katz, *Tradition and Crisis* (above, n. 6), 144–146. (See above, page 23, note 12 for a full citation.)

alternative interests and sources of identity in various spiritual and economic contexts – or even initiate divorces – these channels were unavailable to young women, whose lives were confined to a framework dictated by the hegemonic force of the traditional patriarchal order.[7]

This social order and the power structure it embodied precluded any possibility of free choice or personal decision-making and generally took no account of feelings of love and affection, attraction or revulsion, willingness or refusal. It allowed for no open, flexible framework within which marriages might be established or dissolved on the basis of the equal choice of the interested parties. And so there developed various ways for escaping these oppressive social conventions. Those individuals who could not respond to society's demands and expectations with respect to their partners and could not express their feelings, and those who were unable to satisfy their desires in the accepted ways, turned to various ways of avoiding the expectations and fleeing the duties imposed by the oppressive social order.

---

[7] On the significance of the patriarchal order for women's lives, see Rachel Elior, "'*Nokheḥot nifkadot,' 'teva domem,' ve-'almah yafah she-ein lah einayim': li-she'elat nokheḥutan ve-he'adran shel nashim, bi-leshon ha-kodesh, ba-dat ha-yehudit, u-va-meẓi'ut ha-yisra'elit*" (On the question of women's presence and absence in the Hebrew language, the Jewish religion, and Israeli society). *Alpayyim* 20 (2000), 214–270 (portions translated into English by Rachelle Avital as "'Present but Absent,' 'Still Life' and 'A Pretty Maiden Who Has No Eyes': On the Presence and Absence of Women in the Hebrew Language, in Jewish Culture and in Israeli Life," in Elḥanan Reiner and Rachel Livneh-Freudenthal, eds., *Streams Into the Sea: Studies in Jewish Culture and Its Context, Dedicated to Felix Posen.* Tel Aviv: Alma, 2001, 191–211); Grossman, *Pious and Rebellious* (above, n. 6), 37–67; Ruth Lamdan, *A Separate People: Jewish Women in Palestine, Syria, and Egypt in the Sixteenth Century.* Boston: Brill, 2000.

The principal way in which powerless people could deviate from the patriarchal order while still remaining within the traditional world was by succumbing to illness, a step that occasionally used the power of physical and mental weakness to gain a degree of distance and liberation from the expected order. The best-known form of illness was that of the "dybbuk," which could serve as an escape route from marital bonds that had been imposed against the will of the interested parties. In the absence of any other way to resist the forces of the hegemonic power structure, the dybbuk allowed for the expression of such resistance, represented by the loss of control over one's mind and body.

In the traditional world, "dybbuk" referred to a state of mental illness and loss of control in which the body is seen, by the patient and those around him or her, to have been infiltrated by a force from beyond it. That force gains control over the body, seizing it relentlessly, causing it to act in an extraordinary and frightening manner, and exempting it from accountability to the usual norms. A person overcome by a dybbuk is characterized as mentally ill, as epileptic, or as having been infiltrated by a dead person's spirit speaking through the victim's mouth as a distinct, foreign personality. As a result, the victim becomes exempt from carrying out the expectations associated with conventional norms. Having been taken over by an uncontrollable force, the victim by his or her very nature transcends accepted human limitations based on boundaries, separations, conventions, and distinct categories.

The essential mysterious nature of mental or psychological illnesses that entail losing control, going out of one's mind, and departing from standard norms in a manner entailing annulment of the accepted social order, remained a frightening enigma. The mysterious phenomenon gave rise to religious, social, and cultural interpretations and to a variety of coping strategies that sought to find justification, meaning, and purpose in the departure from the norm and even to clear a path for returning to it. The dybbuk inspired widespread fear, for its effects could not be controlled, its various manifestations entailed deviance from established norms, and there was an implicit belief that it could not be cured in the way that other mental illnesses could be cured. Nevertheless, traditional society generated attitudinal structures and curative measures based on contextual cultural interpretations, which defined the phenomenon in connection with the concealed world and the domain of demonology and impurity. (The terminology used in alluding to the domain of impurity includes: "wandering spirits" – dybbuk; an evil spirit from the world of the dead entering a living person and clinging to him or to her; "a spirit entered her;" – an illness of the spirit; "a demon entered him" – seizure by external forces.) Although the dybbuk caused uncontrolled personal conduct and entailed altered states of consciousness and deviant behavior, these definitions cast it in traditional interpretive patterns that explained it (spirits, demons, external forces, fiends, dybbuks, husks) and established the community's ritual and curative reactions to the conduct (exorcism of the dybbuk, obtaining help from miracle workers, expelling the external forces, dispatching the demons, adjuring the husk).[8]

---

[8] See Yoram Bilu, "*Ha-dibbuk ba-yahadut: hafra`ah nafshit ke-mash'av tarbuti*" [The dybbuk in Judaism: mental disturbance as cultural resource], in *Meḥkerei yerushalayim be-maḥshevet yisra'el* [*Jerusalem Studies in Jewish Thought*] 2, 4 (1983): 529–563, which includes the literature on culture dependent syndrome and possession trance. See also id., "Dibbuk and Maggid: Two Cultural Patterns of Altered Consciousness in Judaism," *AJS Review* 21 (1996): 341–366 (henceforth: Bilu, "Dibbuk and Maggid"). For comparative study of these forms of conduct, see Erika Bourguignon, *Possession.* San Francisco: Chandler and Sharp, 1976; Matt Goldish, ed., *Spirit Possession in Judaism: Cases and Context – From the Middle Ages to the Present.* Detroit: Wayne State Univ. Press, 2003. For bibliography on the dybbuk, see the entry for the term in *The Catalog of Gershom Scholem Library*

The term "dybbuk," as used in kabbalistic literature and in kabbalistically-inspired popular literature, refers to a psychological state in which one experiences the entrance of a deceased's spirit into the body of a living person. The deceased's spirit – termed "a spirit of impurity," an "evil spirit," a "spirit of the outside forces," a "fiend," a disembodied spirit," or "the soul of one so wicked that his soul cannot enter *Gehinnom* (Gehenna, loosely "hell," but with different overtones) on account of his many sins" – is conceived within the context of punishment and reward, and envisioned as attempting to escape the forces pursuing and tormenting it by penetrating the body of a living person against that person's will, seizing it (hence the term "seizure"), adhering to it (hence the term "dybbuk," literally, "adhesion"), and taking it over (hence the term "possession").[9]

---

of Jewish Mysticism, eds. Joseph Dan, Esther Liebes, and Samuel Re'em, vol. 2. Jerusalem: The National University Library, 1999, 904–906. For recent scholarship on the subject and a comprehensive historical contextualization within the religious and intellectual combats of early modern European history, see Jeffrey Chajes, *Between Worlds: Dybbuks, Exorcists and Early Modern Judaism.* Philadelphia: Univ. of Pennsylvania Press, 2003. The book includes a comprehensive translation appendix of possession texts in English. Cf. Eli Yassif, "*Between Worlds: Dybbuks, Exorcists, and Early Modern Judaism* by J.H. Chajes," *History of Religions* 46/2 (November 2006): 179–184.

[9] The ancient roots of this concept appear as early as the apocryphal book of Tobit, written in the fourth century B.C.E.: "If a devil or an evil spirit trouble any, we must make a smoke thereof before the man or the woman, and the party shall be no more vexed.... And the devil shall smell it and flee away, and never come again any more" (6:17). Several incantations to exorcise demons were found among the Dead Sea Scrolls. Cf. Esther Eshel, "Genres of Magical Texts in the Dead Sea Scrolls," in *Demons: The Demonology of Israelite-Jewish and Early Christian Literature in Context of their Environment [=Die Dämonen: die Dämonologie der israelitisch-jüdischen und frühchristlichen Literatur im Kontext ihrer Umwelt]*, edited by Armin Lange, Hermann Lichtenberger, and K. F. Diethard Romheld, 395–415.

According to various written records, the dybbuk speaks from the mouth of the person possessed as a distinct personality.

Until fairly recently, the medical world classified these phenomena judgmentally – and negatively – as psychological disturbances, mental illness, or a form of hysteria. In contrast, contemporary psychologists and anthropologists have defined them neutrally, in more moderate tones, as altered states of consciousness or as culture-dependent syndromes that can be interpreted in an intelligible cultural context based on the premise that some alien entity infiltrates a person's body, takes control of his body and his soul, and drives his actions.[10] Eyewitness accounts of the phenomenon, written in the sixteenth century and later, see it as threatening and frightening and connect it with epilepsy ("the falling sickness") and with mental illness and madness.[11] Popular tales interpret the phenomenon as

---

Tubingen: Mohr Siebeck, 2003. Spirit possession is mentioned in Josephus, who wrote in the last few decades of the first century C.E. and characterizes the spirits that take control of human bodies as the souls of the wicked: "[a certain plant] has one virtue that makes it sought after; for the so-called devils – in reality the spirits of evil-doers that enter the living and kill them if they are not rescued – are quickly cast out by this plant if it so much as touches the possessed" (Josephus, *The Jewish War*, 7:6:3, trans. G. A. Williamson [New York: Dorset Press by arrangement with Penguin Press, 1985], 388). The New Testament, written in the last several decades of the first century C.E., describes various incidents in which Jesus exorcizes spirits: Mark 1:23–27, 38–39; 7:25–26, 29–30; 9:17–19; and parallel accounts in the other gospels.

[10] Bilu, "*Ha-dibbuk ba-yahadut*" (above, n. 8), 531. In his "Dibbuk and Maggid" (above, n. 8), Bilu notes that the dybbuk was generally regarded as causing mental illness and hysterical phenomena.

[11] For a collection of these accounts, see Gedaliah Nigal, *Sippurei dibbuk be-sifrut yisra'el* (*Dybbuk Tales in Jewish Literature*). Jerusalem: Reuben Mass, 1983; 2nd ed., 1994. Cf. id., "*Ha-dibbuk ba-mistikah ha-yehudit*" (The dybbuk in Jewish mysticism). *Da'at* 4 (1980): 75–101. For English translation Cf. Chajes, *Between*

the result of being seized by a demon, of magic, or of infiltration by a spirit.[12] Modern historians suggest a range of interpretations that examine the inter-religious cultural context of dybbuks and their exorcism, tied to the demonization of the world in the early modern period in reaction to the critical and significant changes taking place at the time.[13] Investigators of

---

Worlds (above, n. 8), appendix of possession stories. On the authenticity of these accounts, see below, nn. 46–47. On their place in folk religion and on the tension between historical and fictional representations see Yassif, "*Between Worlds*" (above, n. 8), 181–184. Scholars assume that literary reworkings of traditions grounded in oral accounts contain authentic elements. The large number of these traditions attests in itself to a kernel of truth and an authentic context; beyond that, the medical dimensions of the reports of exorcism and cure and their fixed interpretive context afford them a historical aspect that augments their reliability.

[12] Sarah Tzfatman, "*Ma`aseh shel ruaḥ be-k.k. Kareẓ: shelav ḥadash be-hitpatḥut shel zhenre amami*" (A spirit tale in the holy community of Koretz: a new stage in the development of a folk genre). *Meḥkerei yerushalayim be-folklor yehudi* (*Jerusalem Studies in Jewish Folklore*) 2 (1982): 17–65; id., "*Gerush ruḥot ra'ot bi-perag ba-me'ah ha–17: li-she'eilat meihemnuto ha-historit shel zhenre amami*" (Exorcism of evil spirits in Prague during the seventeenth century: on the historical reliability of a folk genre). Id., 3 (1982): 7–34. Chajes's work, mentioned in the notes above and below, contributes to the appreciation of dybbuk stories as an important chapter in the history of magic.

[13] Daniek Pickering Walker, *Unclean Spirits: Possession and Exorcism in France and England in the Late Sixteenth and Early Seventeenth Centuries* (Philadelphia: Scholars Press, 1981); H.C. Eric Midelfort, "The Devil and the German People: Reflections on the Popularity of Demon Possession in Sixteenth-Century Germany," in *Religion and Culture in the Renaissance and Reformation: Sixteenth-Century Essays and Studies* 11 (1989): 99–119; J.H. Chajes, "Judgment Sweetened: Possession and Exorcism in Early Modern Jewish Culture," *Journal of Early Modern History* 1, 2 (1997): 124–162; id., "Spirit Possession and the Construction of Early Modern Jewish Religiosity (doctoral dissertation, Yale Univ., 1993), now published as *Between Worlds: Dybbuks, Exorcists, and Early Modern Judaism*

traditional socio-religious culture explain the dybbuk phenomenon in the context of relationships between the strong and weak, in which the ability to control the body and bring it to a state in which it lacks self-control and rejects and breaches norms represents the only power of the otherwise powerless.

Gedaliah Nigal collected eighty stories about dybbuks and reports of their exorcism that he had found in varied Jewish sources from the sixteenth century to today, publishing them in his work *"Dybbuk": Tales in Jewish Literature* (see n. 11). In his preface to the collection, he provides a detailed account of the stories' literary genre and cultural background. Nigal's findings suggest that it was not uncommon for women who did not know how to speak about themselves and their psychological anguish, and who were not heard in public, to express themselves through physical ailments, mental afflictions, and associated madness.[14] The body possessed

---

(Philadelphia: University of Pennsylvania Press, 2003). Chajes points out that stories on possession as well as other evidence of supernatural appearances, such as spirits and demons, were abroad in the Christian community as well as in the Jewish community, serving as weaponry in the great seventeenth-century combat against rationalistic tendencies and the move to abandon belief in the eternity of the souls and punishment after death.

[14] Phyllis Chesler argues that madness is a choice made by a woman who cannot or is unwilling to tread the normative path and act in the way a woman is expected to act. Phyllis Chesler, *Women and Madness* (Garden City, NY: Doubleday, 1972). Cf. Sandra M. Gilbert and Susan Gubar, *The Madwoman in the Attic* (New Haven and London: Yale Univ. Press, 1979), index entries for "madness" and "disease." Chesler's comments – "Women who reject or are ambivalent about the female role frighten both themselves and society so much so that their ostracism and self-destructiveness probably begin very early" (*Women and Madness*, 56) and "Young women are sent to die in marriage, motherhood and madness" (id., 297) – are remarkably illustrated in Bracha Serri's story *"Keri`ah,"* which tells of a very young girl, innocent of all sexual knowledge, whose family gives her against her

by a dybbuk is represented as being under the control of the chaotic world of the dead, which imposes higher claims on it than does the patriarchal world of real life, and the person possessed is thereby liberated from the latter. By superseding the usual circle of social expectations and proper conduct, the dybbuk could offer, to those unwilling or unable to accept the social dictates associated with matchmaking, marriage, enforced sexual relations, and family, a justification for conduct that deviated from religious, sexual, or social norms.[15]

Scholars have noted that the dybbuk is an individual manifestation of an "institutional" disturbance, grounded in an on-going collective myth; it thereby differs from contemporary psychiatric disturbances, which are grounded in an individual myth that reflects a unique, non-shared pathology. Yoram Bilu pointed out that the dybbuk phenomenon can appear only in a traditional and cohesive society having a formulated

---

will in an arranged marriage to an aged widower. Under the guise of ritually obligatory intercourse he rapes her on their wedding night, and she goes mad. The madness is presented as the only way in which she can escape and raise her voice – the voice of one coerced, cruelly oppressed, and violently raped, all within the "normal" conventional social framework of her community. See Bracha Serri, "*Keri`ah*" (Tearing). In *Ha-kol haaḥer: sipporet nashim ivrit* (*The Other Voice*), edited by Lily Rattok, 35–50. Tel Aviv: Ha-Kibbutz ha-Me'uḥad, ha-Sifryah ha-Ḥadashah, Sifrei Siman Keri'ah, 1994). First published in 1980 in the first volume of *Nogah*, a feminist review; in 1987, this dreadful story was made into a play and staged at the Beit Ariella Theater in Tel Aviv. Yemenite-Jewish men protested the play in a petition to the President of Israel and in demonstrations at the theater, but Yemenite-Jewish women argued that their misery was far more intense in reality than that depicted in the play. See Hannah Safran, *Lo roẓot lihyot neḥmadot: ha-ma'avak al zekhut ha-beḥirah le-nashim ve-reshito shel ha-feminizm he-ḥadash be-yisra'el* [*Don't Wanna Be Nice Girls: The Struggle for Suffrage and the New Feminism in Israel*] (Haifa: Pardes, 2006), 127–128.

[15] Elior, *Nokheḥot nifkadot* (above, n. 7), 258–260.

cosmology and a system of norms that effectively regulate the conduct of its members.[16]

The dybbuk drew its inspiration from a collective myth within traditional Jewish society, a myth grounded in a set of beliefs adhered to by the community. The community believed in a sanctified norm that mediated between the hidden and the revealed; in reward and punishment that transcended the borders of life and death; in the transmigration of souls; in the existence of spirits and demons; and in a permeable boundary between the world of the dead and the world of the living.[17] That boundary is subject to being breached in situations of illness and crisis, when madness bridges the revealed and the hidden worlds, blurring the lines between the world of humans and the world of spirits and demons from the impure realm. The dybbuk may be a voicing of an individual's concrete suffering, but the believing society interprets it in a communal context, bound up in concepts of reward and punishment and in terms of "entry" and "exit" – that is, possession by and exorcism of the dybbuk. The concrete suffering implicit in the victim's story, expressed in the breaching of physical and mental boundaries and the loss of control over body and soul, becomes part of a complex socio-religious process that draws from the illness lessons regarding the fate – transcending boundaries of time and place – of those who breach the restraints of propriety.

The accounts in Jewish sources of dybbuks and their exorcism show that the illness, for the most part, afflicts people who have been

---

[16] Bilu, "*Ha-dibbuk ba-yahadut*" (above, n. 8), 559. See also id., "Dibbuk and Maggid."

[17] For examples of the living reality of this collective myth, as reflected in folk tales, see Eli Yassif, *The Hebrew Folktale: History, Genre, Meaning*, trans. from the Hebrew by Jacqueline S. Teitelbaum. Bloomington: Indiana University Press, 1999, 351–370, 529–531.

marginalized by society. The victim's implicit story pertains to anxiety over undesired matches, compelled marriages, rape, incest, or bodily or psychological compulsion of the weak by the strong. Such instances of compulsion, tied to multi-layered physical and symbolic feelings of powerlessness, speechlessness and the associated anxiety, generate reactions that are expressed through a loss of control over body and soul, bound up in a dramatic alteration of consciousness termed a "dybbuk."

Contexts for the Dybbuk

In its first biblical appearance, the stem *d-b-k* refers to the pairing of a man and a woman: "Therefore shall a man leave his father and his mother, and shall cling [*ve-davak*] to his wife, and they shall be one flesh" (Gen. 2:24). The self-evident connection between ownership (*ba'alut*) and sexual intercourse (*be'ilah*) – "When a man takes a wife and possesses her [*u-ve'alah*], and it happens that she does not please him, for he finds something unseemly in her, and he writes her a bill of divorcement and sends her out of his house…." (Deut. 24:1)[18] – is evident to this day in such terms as *ba'al* (husband), *ba'ali* (my husband), *bo'el* (a man engaging in intercourse with a woman), and *be'ilah shel mizvah* (intercourse obligatory for the fulfillment of a commandment). Obligatory intercourse in a milieu of sanctity and purity is a social convention that embodies the hegemonic power structure's symbolic-cultural order with regard to the body and its ownership. That conventional order, within the limits defined by taboos, is described in biblical Hebrew by two verbs – *b-'-l* and *d-b-k*. In contrast, forbidden intercourse, in a milieu of menstrual uncleanliness, impurity,

[18] See also BT *Yevamot* 5a.

incest, or rape, breaches the bounds of the taboo. What is legally forbidden takes place in practice, and the hopelessness it engenders in one forced against his or her will to endure these relations may come to be expressed by breaching the bounds of body and soul in the manner referred to as "dybbuk."

"Bonding [*devekut*] of the flesh," or permitted intercourse, entails a consensual, covenantal breach of bodily boundaries. It is safeguarded by the social order, by laws and taboos, and by the sanctity of marriage; but it sometimes becomes transformed, in non-consensual situations, into bonding – *dibbuk* – that involves a rape or the forced penetration of a living body by a deceased's spirit. According to the various narrative traditions pertaining to the dybbuk, the penetration frequently takes place via the genitalia, and the usual sexual analogue is rape.[19] Often, the dybbuk is described in terms of *ibbur* ("impregnation"),[20] a term with an obvious affinity to intercourse and pregnancy; and *ibbur* is the earlier term for the

---

[19] On the entry of the spirit as rape, see Bilu, "*Ha-dibbuk ba-yahadut*" (above, n. 8), 540; Nigal, *Sippurei dibbuk* (above, n. 10), 175, 207. On entry of the spirit via the genitals, see Nigal, id., 27, 34, 63, 65, 179, 211; Bilu, id., 540–542, 545.

[20] On impregnation in relation to transmigration and dybbuk, see Gershom Scholem, "The Transmigration of Souls," in *On the Mystical Shape of the Godhead*, trans. from the German by Joachim Neugroschel, edited and revised by Jonathan Chipman (New York: Schocken Books, 1991), 221–223, 306. The concept is derived from the soul's passage from body to body and from *ibbur* in the sense of impregnation. Scholem cites the expression *ibbur ra* ("evil impregnation"), "in which the soul of a wicked person entered the body of a living person who had allowed it to enter by committing some serious transgression. While the *ibbur* of the righteous soul is revealed in a heightening of the personality and a strengthening of its good tendencies the 'evil *ibbur*' can destroy the personality entirely: 'And that soul was impregnated within him, to strengthen him in his wickedness, until he passed away from the world'" (id., 223). Cf. Ẓevi Hirsch Koidonover, *Kav ha-yashar* (Frankfurt a/M 1705), chapter 40.

entry of a spirit into a person's body that later comes to be described as a dybbuk. At times the phenomenon is depicted as "Hysteria," an illness clearly associated with female sexuality and involving psychological protest and deviance from the conventions of the social order with regard to ownership of that sexuality. "Hysteria" is derived from the Greek word for womb, *hystera,* and its connection, in its social and biological meaning, to women's sexuality and their control over their bodies is unavoidable.[21] Nevertheless, it seems almost never to have been considered from this perspective in studies of the dybbuk.[22] One who experiences the basic state

---

[21] Ron Barkai, "*Masorot refu'iyot yevaniyot ve-hashpa`atan al tefisat ha-ishah bi-yemei ha-beinayyim*" (Greek Medical Traditions and their Impact on Conceptions of Women in the Gynecological Writings in the Middle Ages). In *A View into the Lives of Women in Jewish Societies: Collected Essays,* edited by Yael Azmon, 128. Jerusalem: 1995.

[22] In Greek culture and later in Medieval Latin literature, the womb is described as a living entity having a will of its own and roaming independently through the woman's body, giving rise thereby to various ailments. Plato described the womb as an entity having desires, primarily to carry the fetus: "... when remaining unfruitful long beyond its proper time, [the womb] gets disconnected and angry, and wandering in every direction through the body, closes up the passages of the breath, and, by obstructing respiration, drives them to extremity, causing all varieties of disease" (*Timaeus* 91C, in *The Dialogues of Plato*, trans. into English by B. Jowett, with an introduction by Raphael Demos. New York: Random House, 1937, vol. 2, 67). The wandering womb was taken in Hippocratic and Galenic texts to explain the phenomenon of "strangulated womb" or hysteria. See Ron Barkai, "*Masorot refu'iyot yevaniyot ve-hashpa'atan al tefisat ha-ishah bi-yemei ha-beinayyim*" (Greek medical traditions and their influence on the understanding of women in the Middle Ages), in *Eshnav le-ḥayyeihen shel nashim be-ḥevrot yehudiyot* (*A View Into the Lives of Women in Jewish Societies*), ed. Yael Azmon, 127–128. Jerusalem: Merkaz Zalman Shazar, 1995. On hysteria, almost invariably listed among women's illnesses, cf. the definitions of Joseph Raulin in the eighteenth century and of Thomas Willis, a seventeenth-century physician, both

quoted in Michel Foucault, *Madness and Civilization: A History of Insanity in the Age of Reason*, trans. from the French by Richard Howard (New York: Random House, 1965). The former writes that "This disease in which women invent, exaggerate, and repeat all the various absurdities of which a disordered imagination is capable, has sometimes become epidemic and contagious" (id., 138–139). According to the latter, "Among the diseases of women, hysterical affection is of such bad repute that like the *semi-damnati* it must bear the faults of numerous other affections; if a disease of unknown nature and hidden origin appears in a woman in such a manner that its cause escapes us, and that the therapeutic course is uncertain, we immediately blame the bad influence of the uterus, which, for the most part, is not responsible, and when we are dealing with an inhabitual symptom, we declare that there is a trace of hysteria hidden beneath it all, and what has so often been the subterfuge of so much ignorance we take as the object of our treatment and our remedies" (id., 137–138). Foucault interprets Willis to mean that the concept of hysteria is a catch-all not for the patient's delusions but for those of the ignorant physician, who presumes to know why this person is ill. On the medical view of the hysterical woman, which illustrates that critique, see Foucault, id., 139–152. On the concept of the womb in medieval medicine and the resulting fate of women, see Ron Barkai, "*Tefisot ginekologiyot bi-yemei ha-beinayim u-ve-reishit ha-et ha-ḥadashah*" (Medieval and early modern gynecological concepts). in *Mada, magiyah, u-mitologiyah bi-yemei ha-beinayim* (*Science, Magic, and Mythology in the Middle Ages*). Jerusalem: Van Leer Institute, 1987, 37–56. Barkai's inquiry into gynecological concepts and women's illnesses provides remarkable illustrations of Foucault's ideas. They link the theoretical discourse about madness and the social attitude toward the insane of both sexes to a broad complex of cultural norms, power relationships, institutional frameworks, and forms of discussion. The Jewish medical tradition in the sixteenth century and later regarded hysteria, dybbuk, madness, and mental illness under a single rubric. In his book *Oẓar ha-ḥayyim* (Venice, 1583), which considers afflictions of body and mind, the Jewish physician Jacob Zahalon examines "folly of the womb," hysteria. The physician Tobias ben Moses Cohen, in the section of his *Ma`aseh Tuviyah* (Venice, 1708) devoted to women's illnesses (*Gan na`ul*), describes the link between the womb and the dybbuk, referred to as "strangulation of the womb": "Strangulation of the womb of hysteria – dissociation – is a broken person, void of all feeling. From a psychological point of view, hysteria is described as a state in which a person's level of self-criticism approaches zero and the person therefore can easily be influenced. The hysterical person tries to preserve a myth of passivity, that is, to avoid all responsibility for his or her internally generated thoughts, impulses, and actions; and he or she does so by identifying with the dominant images in the culture.

Of particular interest is the use in rabbinic Hebrew of the word *kever* (usually "grave") to mean "womb." Giving birth is described by the phrase "as long as the 'grave' is open," and a woman who has given birth is considered unclean for forty or eighty days, depending on the sex of the child (*Mishnah*, *Ohalot* 7:4).[23] One can see here the ambivalence and

---

may befall women, with several terrible and dreadful effects. Its signs are cessation of breathing, epilepsy, shaking of the limbs, fainting, coldness of the extremities, croaking sounds, and stomach distress from spirits that are confined within and circulate through the various parts of the body. Sometime, poisonous vapors go up to the head, and they appear as if dead." Suggested remedies include: "First, correct all acidification within her. Second, expel the spirits to the outside. Third, open the veins. Fourth, remove the wound that is found" (Chapter 7, 120). On the characterization of the dybbuk within the context of hysteria and its conception as a clear example of an illness that attempts to preserve the myth of passivity, see Bilu, "*Ha-dibbuk ba-yahadut*" (above, n. 8), 561–562 and nn. 75 and 167 (including earlier literature). See also id., "The Taming of the Deviants and Beyond: An Analysis of Dybbuk Possession and Exorcism in Judaism." In Goldish, *Spirit Possession* (above, n. 8), 65–66. Bilu there considers hysteria in light of Krohn's observations on the myth of passivity on the part of those possessed by dybbuks. Alan Krohn, *Hysteria: The Elusive Neurosis*. New York: International Universities Press, 1978.

[23] Cf. the definitions of *reḥem* and *kever* in the Ben-Yehudah and Even-Shoshan dictionaries. In his *Commentary on the Mishnah*, ad loc., Maimonides writes that "'the *kever* is opened' is a term for the opening of the womb, used in that way

anxiety regarding the powerful forces of life and death associated with a woman's body, with the cycles of fertility and destruction reflected in it, and with how those cycles relate to the limits of ownership of and dominion over that body in the context of purity and impurity, approach and withdrawal. The purity or impurity of a woman's body is associated with the womb and with the menstrual blood that flows from it in an uncontrollable cycle that sets the bounds of sexual approach and withdrawal with reference to the symbols of life (purity, coupling, potential procreation) and death (impurity, menstruation, potential destruction). It follows that, from a woman's perspective the dybbuk established a state of symbolic impurity that forbade physical contact on account of the spirit's origin in the untamed, impure, chaotic world of the dead.

In the traditional Jewish conception, death in all its manifestations – symbolic and metaphoric no less than actual and concrete – is the primal

---

throughout the Talmud." The medical literature's attitude toward women rests not infrequently on Aristotle's explanations, and his stereotypical generalizations about women's bodies and minds were widely accepted until modern times: "Woman is more compassionate than man, more easily moved to tears, and at the same time is more jealous, more querulous, and more apt to scold and to strike. She is, furthermore, more prone to despondency and less hopeful than man, more void of shame, more false of speech, more deceptive, and of more retentive memory. She is also more wakeful, more shrinking, more difficult to rouse to action, and requires a smaller amount of nutriment.... The male is more courageous than the female, and more sympathetic in the way of standing by to help." (Aristotle, *History of Animals*, in *Complete Works of Aristotle – The Revised Oxford Translation*, ed. Jonathan Barnes. Princeton: Princeton Univ. Press, 1984, vol. 1, 949.) See Barkai, "*Masorot refu'iyot yevaniyot*" (above, n. 21), 124. Barkai cites additional generalizations of this sort, based on religious truths in the Muslim world, holding that "Gehinnom is populated primarily by women" and "The best of women are licentious, the degenerate among them are simply harlots… they complain that they are oppressed when, in fact, they are the oppressors" (id., 122).

source of impurity, ousting anything in its proximity from the pure domain of the living. Accordingly, a body infiltrated by a dead or unclean spirit becomes impure and untouchable on the associative, cultural-symbolic plane. As already noted, "possession" refers to the body being taken hold of by the spirit that penetrates it, by compulsion or other coerced intercourse, and being transferred against its will from the domain of the living to the domain of the dead. In more than a few instances, the violent breach of the spiritual boundaries between the domains of life and death, extensively described in the dybbuk stories, reflects the violent breach of the boundaries between bodies, which is passed over in silence.[24]

The stories about dybbuks and the reports of their exorcism, all of them told from a masculine perspective, make no attempt to probe the social circumstances that influence the development of the illness. Instead, they interpret it in arbitrary mystical or biological contexts – the entry of a deceased person's spirit or "madness of the womb." But the dybbuk's connection with hysteria (from the Greek word for "womb," as already noted) and with the root *d-b-k* (related in biblical Hebrew to copulation, again as noted) indicates the semantic field on which we must interpret the phenomenon and seek its significance.

In the later, Freudian concept, it is repressed libidinal impulses that give rise to hysterical symptoms. An analysis of the dybbuk accounts, in contrast, shows that the illness's various manifestations are tied not to the repression of desire but to the escape from terrifying, repulsive experiences

---

[24] See Grossman, "Prostitution and Concubinage," in *Pious and Rebellious* (above, n. 6), 133–147. For an examination of various aspects forbidden and coerced relations, see Elimelekh Horowitz, "*Bein adonim le-mesharetim ba-ḥevrah ha-yehudit be-eropah bein yemei ha-beinayim le-reishit ha-et ha-ḥadashah*" (Between masters and maidservants in medieval and early modern European Jewish society). In *Eros, eirusin ve-issurim* (above, n. 5), edited by Bartal and Gafni, 193–211.

and from coercion. Bilu's definition of the dybbuk shows the influence of the later Freudian idea, which sees hysteria as "an expression of forbidden desires and impulses in the context of the Possession Trance idiom, which makes it possible to situate them in some external entity alien to the ego – that is, the spirit" or considers it "on the premise that the actions of the spirit represent the woman's repressed sexual fantasies." In that light, Bilu regards the dybbuk as "an expression of impulses and desires that give rise to conflict… or to the projection of repressed impulses onto an external entity (even if it is situated within the person), that is, the infiltrating spirit."[25] Bilu makes no reference here to the opposite possibility, which strikes me as clearly implied by many of the dybbuk stories – and as not all that distant from Freud's original definition of the factors that cause hysteria. In an 1896 lecture entitled "The Aetiology of Hysteria," Freud determined that hysterical women and girls were the victims of cruel sexual exploitation in their childhood or youth: "… at the bottom of every case of hysteria there are one or more occurrences of premature sexual experience, occurrences which belong to the earliest years of childhood…."[26]

Accounts of dybbuk exorcisms and clinical assessments of hysteria suggest that the spirit may serve simultaneously as an expression of the torments, terrors, and sexual coercion passed over in silence and

---

[25] Bilu, *Ha-dibbuk ba-yahadut* (above, n. 8), 537, 542, 538.

[26] Freud, "The Aetiology of Hysteria," in *The Standard Edition of the Complete Psychological Works of Sigmund Freud*, trans. under the editorship of James Strachey. London: The Hogarth Press and the Institute of Psychoanalysis, 1962, vol. 3, 203. Freud's perceptive observations on his suffering female patients as "victims of cruel sexual exploitation in their childhood or youth" were rejected completely by the peaceful residents of Vienna who refused to believe that there is any connection between male sexual coercion and female mental illness. Freud reformulated his original observation under public pressure and reintroduced them in the later Freudian theory as quoted above.

disregarded by society and as almost the only way to escape the yoke of that coercion. Of seventy-five cases documented in dybbuk narratives and exorcism reports, forty-nine involved women suffering from possession by a dybbuk, while only twenty-six involved men.[27] Most of the ill people,

---

[27] See Nigal, *Sippurei dibbuk be-sifrut yisra'el* (above, n. 11), 35, and cf. Chajes, *Between Worlds* (above, n. 8). Nigal notes as well that "of the women, a significant number were young women after their marriages" and that "the abundance of post-marriage young women among the afflicted is a finding that recurs in various cultures" (id.). See also Bilu, *Ha-dibbuq ba-yahadut* (above, n. 8), 541 and n. 55. Bilu notes that cross-cultural studies have shown that women are more inclined than men "to enter into" a "Possession Trance," a state of altered consciousness in which some alien entity is said to have infiltrated a person's body. That finding is so consistent that is may be said to be a universal characteristic of the phenomenon (id., 533–534 and literature there cited). In analyzing the gender breakdown of dybbuk accounts, it becomes clear that the most common case is that of a male spirit entering a female victim (id., 539). Bilu notes as well that "most explanations of the large number of women possessed by dybbuks rely on the safe-harbor assumption according to which women, because of their depressed status in traditional societies, find the Possession Trance to be an easy way to express their frustrations and to flee the difficulties of day-to-day life.... The emphasis is on women in many places being a social category subject to depression and suffering intense role-related pressures" (id., 533–534).

Bilu's doctoral dissertation, "*Psikhiatriyah mesoratit be-yisra'el, peniyot shel benei moshavim yoẓe'ei maroko im be`ayot psikhiatriyot u-keshyei ḥayyim le-rabbanim va-ḥakhamim* (Traditional Jewish psychiatry in Israel – Moroccan immigrants with psychiatric problems turning to rabbis and sages), Jerusalem: 1978, was based on field studies in traditional Jewish settlements in Israel during the 1970s. Bilu notes there that "in our sample, for every man turning for help, there are two women... we are dealing here with a woman's area.... Women are also more vulnerable.... Sixty-two percent have not yet reached their thirties when they seek help" (45–48).

For an up-to-date review of the various positions in anthropological and historical studies regarding cases of spirit infiltration in relation to the social, educational, and sexual discrimination suffered by women, of the "choice" involved in the

regardless of gender, were young, and they came mostly from the lower social classes. Strikingly, a majority of the girls above the age of puberty were brides, young women who had recently been or were about to be married. Ninety percent of the spirits taking possession of the victims were men. Dybbuks, like hysteria, declined markedly or disappeared entirely with the advent of a series of changes in society: a decline in the number of coerced marriages and of servant girls dependent on the goodwill of their masters and subject to their sexual demands; a weakening of the patriarchal order; a change in the accepted view of the woman's role in matters related to marriage and a lessened ability to impose that view by force; the acceptance of open discussion of incest, sexual coercion, exploitation, and rape; and the emergence for women of expanded opportunities for self-expression, free choice, voicing of their concerns and preferences, as well as growing opportunities for self-realization, equality, decision-making, and freedom.

The Dybbuk in the Public Arena

The accounts of dybbuks and reports of their exorcism suggest that the preeminent indicators of infiltration by a spirit are the loss of bodily control and the sounding of an alien voice within a familiar body. As the ill person

---

syndrome, and of the feminine "use" of the possession syndrome, see Hayyot (Chajes), "*Mistika'iyot yehudiyot*" (above, n. 4, 159–161). See also Maurice Faierstein, "Maggidim, Spirits and Women in Rabbi Ḥayyim Vital's Book of Visions," in Goldish, ed., *Spirit Possession in Judaism* (above, n. 8), 186–196; Tamar Alexander, "Love and Death in a Contemporary Dybbuk Story: Personal Narrative and the Female Voice," in id., 307–345. Both of these articles are devoted to the distinctive characteristics of dybbuks and women in past and present.

lies dormant, appearing to be asleep or dead and lacking control over his or her body, a voice not the patient's own emanates from his or her throat, convincing those who hear it that the spirit of a deceased person – a dybbuk – is speaking and dramatizing the weighty association between the domains of the living and of the dead. Primary attention, however, appears to be directed not to the speech of the deceased person in control but to the loss of bodily control on the part of the living person, who now finds herself in an altered state of consciousness marked by dissociation from any feeling and by breaches of imposed norms.

This altered state of consciousness is sometimes referred to as loss of sensation, hysteria, or epilepsy, and sometimes as psychic illness, mental illness, or refilling of the emptied consciousness with the voice speaking through it. It is taken to be a breach of the social order, a challenge to the norm, a disruption in need of correction, a deviation in need of amendment generating return to the norm, or an illness in need of cure. Because the source of the illness is understood to be supernatural – the infiltration of a living body by a deceased person's spirit – its cure likewise takes place along the boundary between concrete reality and the supernatural realm in which the members of the community believe. The curative process, carried out in the public domain, aims to repair the disruption and restore the pre-existing order. Within the traditional world, the process is explained in a mystical and magical context, tied to kabbalistic psychological doctrines that associate the human body and soul with the connection between the hidden and revealed domains and between the worlds of the deceased and of the living.

Kabbalistic psychology – based on the soul's life transcending the limits of the body's life, on the existence of the soul both before the creation of the body and after its demise, and on the movement between interchangeable souls and bodies – devoted considerable attention to transmigration as a response to the question of just rewards and punishments.[28] The belief that the souls of the dead were reincarnated in the bodies of the living is mentioned as early as the time of Sa`adia Ga'on, in the tenth century C.E., and is discussed in the first kabbalistic book *Sefer ha-bahir* (The Book of Luminosity), in the twelfth century. The belief may have been renewed and reinvigorated in the early modern period, at the time of the expulsion from Spain, as a sort of compensation for the harsh sense of loss associated with the expulsion, with the destruction of communities, and with the suffering of the exiles who had lost their children and relatives.[29] The increased belief in transmigration had two aspects: On the one hand, it was believed that the souls of those who had been killed – regarded as "righteous ones" bound in the "bond of life" in Paradise, in the domain of the pure – were reincarnated in pure newborns. At the same time, it was believed that the souls of the "impure" wicked, caught in "the catapult" in the impure realm of Gehenna, were reincarnated in bodies possessed by a dybbuk.

Within this context of reward and punishment, the ritual for exorcising a dybbuk was construed to be a settling of the community's accounts with souls that had transgressed against it and impaired its sacred values. The sinners, who had avoided punishment during their lifetimes, were brought,

---

[28] See Rachel Elior, "Soul, Nefesh: The Jewish Doctrine of the Soul." In *Contemporary Jewish Religious Thought,* edited by Arthur A. Cohen and Paul Mendes-Flohr, 887–896. New York: Scribner, 1987.

[29] See Joseph Hacker, "*Ga'on ve-dika'on: ketavim be-havvayatam ha-ruḥanit ve-ha-ḥevratit shel yoẓe'ei sefarad u-portugal be-imperiyah ha-otmanit*" [Pride and depression: polarities in the spiritual and social existence of Spanish and Portuguese exiles in the Ottoman Empire], in *Tarbut ve-ḥevrah be-toledot yisra'el bi-yemei ha-beinayim* [*Culture and Society in Medieval Jewry*], edited by Reuben Bonfil, Menaḥem Ben-Sasson, and Joseph Hacker, 541–586. Jerusalem: Merkaz Zalman Shazar, 1989.

in the form of dead spirits speaking from the throats of the afflicted, before the representatives of the community, who engaged them in a public dialogue. That dialogue followed a fixed ritual, based on a written text and a structured set of expectations, reflected in a mystical drama that used the medium of the illness to forge a link between the domains of the living and the dead. The dybbuk's whisperings were a supernatural event demonstrating the existence, beyond quotidian life, of a different reality in which dark forces were at play. Those forces were governed by established rules understood by the dybbuk's exorcist, who summons to his aid the belief in divine providence and in the power that imposes reward and punishment beyond the bounds of time and space.

On the communal plane, possession by and exorcism of a dybbuk served as a public reinforcement of the social structure and as a ceremonial, communal realization of the concealed system of justice involving other-worldly reward and punishment in the context of transmigration.[30] This embodiment of the social-mystical values of reward and punishment transcending the tangible presumed that the soul had a life beyond the body, both before and after its sojourn within it. Altered states of consciousness and loss of physical and mental control provided an opportunity to manifest the link to the concealed world, the world of the

[30] On transmigration, see Scholem, "The Transmigration of Souls" (above, n. 20), 197–250, 300–312; Rachel Elior, "The doctrine of Transmigration in *Galya Raza*," in *Essential Papers on Kabbalah,* edited by Lawrence Fine, 243–269. New York: New York Univ. Press, 1995; id., *Galya raza: hoẓa'ah bikortit al pi kitvei yad* (*Galya raza*: a critical edition based on the mss.). Jerusalem: Hebrew University, 1981; Moshe Ḥallamish, *An Introduction to the Kabbalah*, trans. from the Hebrew by Ruth Bar-Ilan and Ora Wiskind-Elper. Albany: State Univ. of New York Press, 1999, 75–86. For a list of studies and sources on transmigration, see the entry "*Gilgul*" in the Catalogue of the Gershom Scholem Library of Jewish Mysticism, 901–902 (note 8 above).

souls and of the dead, and to demonstrate publicly the long-range mechanisms of justice, tied to the exile and redemption of souls.

The process for restoring order was intended not only to expel the deceased soul from the living body that it had taken over and merged with but also to return it, even if against its will, to the world of the dead from which it had come. Having emerged uninvited from the domain of impurity and death, this alien entity had penetrated the land of the living, in which it had no proper place; now it was to be expelled in a dramatic public ritual that restores the lines between different sorts of entities and different domains. In effect, two things occur simultaneously in the ritual. First, the community's representatives engage the deceased's spirit, heard through the living body, in conversation. In so doing, they reinforce, publicly and ceremoniously, the bounds of the normal and settle outstanding accounts with those who had transgressed against the community's fundamental values and had acted disloyally, offending against the communal sense of justice.[31] At the same time, the person possessed by a dybbuk undergoes an

[31] Tzfatman's article, "*Gerush ruḥot ra'ot bi-perag*" (above, n. 12), provides an example of such an account-settling dialogue between exorcist and spirit; in it, the spirit that brought about the imprisonment of Rabbi Loewe (Maharal) of Prague is identified. An example of statements by the spirit that pertain to reward and punishment can be found in *Kehal ḥasidim*: "No one saw the deceased except the litigant and the rabbi, but all the people heard his voice. Afterward, the deceased wept and shouted, 'Woe to him who imagines that all will be well with him when he lies in his grave and does not examine his actions in this world, for his end will be bitter." See *Kehal ḥasidim* (Lemberg, 1860), 109. According to Tzfatman-Bieler, "It therefore may be fair to assume that the transformation of a person into a spirit was a special form of punishment, in which the community punished an individual who has transgressed against it and, for various reasons, had not been properly punished, at least as it saw matters. On this understanding, the significance of the spirit's appearance should be examined as a problem flowing from the relationships between the community and the transgressing individual who had become a spirit,

experience of separation from the body and from the social conventions associated with it. Once liberated from the established norms regarding the right to speak or be silent, the possessed person gains, through participation in the ritual, a voice previously denied him or her. From the community's perspective, what is involved is the battle of holiness against impurity, of life against death, of order against chaos, and of norm against deviance.

In traditional, patriarchal societies, women lacked – and still lack – the right to speak in the public domain, a realm subject to male hegemony. They likewise had no authority to contest existing laws or social arrangements that subjected the body to the hegemonic and oppressive religious or cultural order. Women lacked (and many still lack) the right to marry or to decline an arranged marriage, to dissolve the marital bond, or to choose, as they see fit, between entering an actual levirate marriage (*yibbum*) and avoiding it through its purely ceremonial alternative (*ḥaliẓah*).[32] One of the few ways of securing release from this normative straitjacket was by entering, unconsciously or semi-consciously, into a state involving loss of control over the body – a state of possession by a dybbuk. That unique situation produced extraordinary circumstances allowing the ill person to be heard, though in other, more normal circumstances, she would

---

and not necessarily as an internal psychological problem of the ill person.... It may be that the ill person infiltrated by the spirit should not, in essence, be regarded as central or independent factor but should be seen only as a medium, through which the community imposes a sort of sanction on its members."

[32] See Elior, "'*Nokheḥot nifkadot*'" (above, n. 7), 224–230. For historical expressions of these sentiments, see Azmon, ed., *Eshnav le-ḥayyeihen shel nashim* (above, n. 21). On the legal significance, see Frances Raday, Carmel Shalev and Michal Liban-Koby, eds., "*Ma'amad ha-ishah ba-ḥevrah u-va-mishpat* (*Women's Status in Israeli Law and Society*). Jerusalem and Tel-Aviv: Schocken, 1995; R. Elior (ed.) *Men and Women: On Gender Judaism and Democracy*. Jerusalem: Van Leer Institute and Urim Publications, 2004.

be absolutely forbidden to sound a voice in the sacred, masculine public domain. The loss of control was interpreted as an illness that placed its victim in the domain of impurity and death, and the strange voice was interpreted as a dybbuk, a voice from the world of the dead. Together, they transferred the woman possessed by the dybbuk from the domain of purity to the domain of impurity and removed her body, at least temporarily, from the physical, sensory union and coupling that she did not desire. In other words, they suspended the undesired sexual tie or the consummation of the marriage imposed against the will of the woman, liberating her from the social order's institutions.

The various manifestations of the illness – convulsions, agonized moaning, fevers, outbursts, indistinct voices, hysteria, extraordinary behavior, growling, and speaking in unclear, incomplete sentences[33] – or the various manifestations of the abnormal were talked about and recast by the communal representatives participating in the exorcism ritual, who took it upon themselves to formulate clearly what was heard in accord with the community's needs.

From the community's perspective, the dybbuk, which disrupts the bounds of the norm and is always understood as the infiltration of a living body by a dead spirit, is a link between the world of the living and the world of the dead. Embodying a public moral lesson going beyond the bounds of time and place, the abnormal phenomenon serves as a bridge between the revealed and the concealed: between the inadequacies of the revealed world, in which there is no easy settling of accounts regarding justice and injustice, reward and punishment, and the infinite power of the

---

[33] For detailed portrayals, see the exorcism accounts collected in Nigal, *Sippurei dibbuk* (above, n. 11). Cf. Chajes, *Between Worlds* (above, n. 8); Raphael Patai, "Exorcism and Xenoglossia among the Safed Kabbalists," *Journal of American Folklore* 91 (1978), 823–835.

hidden world, in which these accounts are settled beyond the limits of time and space. From the perspective of the person possessed, meanwhile, the forced contact with the world of the dead liberates him or her from the yoke of the world of the living; and the abnormal, as it rises up against the norm, makes it possible to breach the established coercive limitations and turn the community's attention to a state of distress that has no other expression and no conventional solution.

The spirit is an emissary from the world of the dead that suspends the order of the world of the living, and the dybbuk's entry undermines the limitations of the existing order and breaches the bounds of time and space. The deceased does not lie at peace in his grave; rather, his spirit wanders among the living. Meanwhile, the living person does not control his or her life; rather, the wandering spirit of the deceased takes control of the victim, transferring the person so possessed from the domain of purity and life to that of impurity and death. That breach of boundaries is bound up in contact with the sacred, concealed realm on the one hand and, on the other, the monstrous, abnormal realm. Both of those domains are defined by their deviance from the rubrics accepted within the human world. A man's spirit in a girl's body, a sinful soul in an innocent body, a male voice in a female body, or a dead soul in a living body – widespread motifs in dybbuk narratives – all constitute an unbearable breach of boundaries.

The Dybbuk and Witchcraft

During the late Middle Ages and early modern period, the Jewish world became intensely conscious of the polarity between exile and redemption. A mystical, dualistic worldview emerged in which the manifestations of exile were associated with evil and the domain of the *sitra aḥra* (the "other side"), while the manifestations of redemption were associated with the good and the domain of the *sitra de-kedusha* (the "holy side"). The abstract expressions and symbolic representations of these two planes, which united the concealed world with the revealed through the experience of exile and the hope for redemption, left their mark on the conceptual world of the Kabbalah and took on a new literary image that exercised broad influence on Jewish culture. Kabbalistic literature set up a dualistic worldview that distinguished between, on the one hand, the forces of holiness, tied to redemption and to the supernal world of eternal life beyond the bounds of time and space, and, on the other, the forces of impurity, tied to exile and the world below, the menacing world of death. The writers of this literature established two sets of interconnected concepts. One set of concepts refers to the impure side, associated with the *sitra aḥra*, evil spirits, externalities, fiends, demons, dybbuks, and the souls of the wicked, sinful deceased. The second set of concepts relates to the pure and holy side, associated with the *sitra de-kedusha*, the *Shekhinah*, holy spirits, angels, *maggidim*, speech of the *Shekhinah*, and bonding with the supernal beings and with kabbalists and righteous people.

Within the Christian world of that period, meanwhile, there developed a polarity between faith and apostasy, respectively represented in the images of the Church and of Satan. Late-fifteenth-century works on Satan and witchcraft – such as *Malleus Maleficarum* [The Witches' Hammer],[34]

[34] Heinrich Kramer and James Sprenger, *The Malleus Maleficarum*, trans. from the Latin by Montague Summers. New York: Oxford University Press, 1971. Between 1487 and 1520, following the work's initial publication in 1486, the work went through fifteen more editions; an additional sixteen editions were printed between 1574 and 1679. A manual pursuant to church law for identifying witches and people possessed by Satan, the book was written by the inquisitor Heinrich Kramer, a Dominican active in Alsace and Bohemia, and Jakob Sprenger, a Dominican inquisitor and theologian active in Germany. Millions of sick people, mostly

very widely disseminated during the sixteenth and seventeenth centuries – treat "possession" as affliction by Satan and claim that it is brought about by witchcraft.[35] A large majority of those accused of witchcraft were women, just as a large majority of possessed by dybbuks were women. The literature on persecution of witches by the Church and its agents clearly assumes that a "possession" entails Satan's entry into a sinner's body in order to speak from his or her throat. That entry was understood as sexual union between Satan and the witch, and the witch's body was even taken to be Satan's refuge. Throughout the sixteenth and seventeenth centuries and into the eighteenth, the Christian world regularly burned witches, who were seen as Satan's allies, as producers of "possession" or as possessed by Satan or by a demon. That practice was the natural consequence of regarding witchcraft as a satanic sin and as the special province of women.[36] The number of victims of the persecution of witches during that

women, were examined in accord with the manual, brought before priests and judges, and sentenced to torture and death by burning at the stake. The justification was that only in that way could their souls be saved on Judgment Day. Christian theologians argued that the soul, partaking of the divine essence, could not itself become ill; accordingly, its deviance attested to the entry into the victim of an evil spirit that had to be expelled. Mental illness became identified with heresy and witchcraft, and psychological syndromes were interpreted in accord with demonological doctrines.

[35] *The Malleus Maleficarum*, 110.

[36] Id., 41–47, 66, 82–84, 124–134. See also the instructive analysis by British historian Hugh R. Trevor-Roper, *The European Witch Craze of the Sixteenth and Seventeenth Centuries.* New York: Harper & Row, 1967. Cf. the in-depth account in Lyndal Roper, *Oedipus and the Devil: Witchcraft, Sexuality and Religion in Early Modern Europe* London and New York: Routledge, 1994; Stuart Clark, *Thinking with Demons: The Idea of Witchcraft in Early Modern Europe.* Oxford: Clarendon Press, 1997; Robin Briggs, *Witches and Neighbors: The Social and Cultural Context of European Witchcraft.* New York: Harper Collins, 1996.

period – a period associated, ironically enough, with humanism, with the Renaissance, and with the beginnings of modernity – has been variously estimated at between three hundred thousand and one million men and women. The appearance of Satan's might through the various forms of mental illness was a matter of interest to the Church, which sought to sharpen the dichotomy between faith and apostasy, as manifested in the dichotomies between the Church's sacred service on the one hand and Satanism and witchcraft on the other and between the respective earthly representations of good and evil – the clergy and witches. Mentally ill people, hysterical women seized by terror, unattached women, epileptics, and depressed or otherwise odd men or women, all of whom failed to act in accord with accepted norms, were regarded as well suited to being penetrated by Satan. Christian theologians, who wanted to use these persecutions in order to enhance the power of the Church, argued that one who did not believe in the existence of Satan and in the reality of witchcraft and demonic possession likewise did not believe in God, the Church, or the Holy Spirit. It followed that enhancing the image of Satan and waging public war against him would therefore aggrandize the Church and reinforce its dominant position. Within Church circles, demonic possession was considered to be a manifestation of Satan and a punishment incurred by a sinner; nevertheless, it did not come within the Church's penal laws. Witchcraft, in contrast, which could bring about a demonic or satanic possession, was treated by the Bible as a capital offense: "Thou shalt not suffer a sorceress to live" (Ex. 22:17). In accordance with the biblical precedent, as interpreted in the New Testament and the Church Fathers' writings, Church law made witchcraft a criminal offense punishable by torture and burning at the stake. Because of that criminal aspect, the reports of witchcraft and of witches casting demonic possession spells or seized by

Satan are, for the most part, legal reports found primarily in Church writings and in the legal literature of the Inquisition.[37]

Jewish dybbuk narratives from the sixteenth century and later present a different picture. Satan is a marginal figure, and the dybbuk is not a concern of earthly criminal law. Jews living under cross or crescent could not adjudicate capital offenses, for they generally lacked autonomy with respect to criminal law. Accordingly, they could not have persecuted witches even if they had wanted to. *The Scroll of Aḥima'aẓ*, written in southern Italy in the eleventh century, includes stories told in the Jewish community of witches who preyed on children. *Sefer ḥasidim*, written in thirteenth-century Ashkenaz (Franco-Germany), attests to the belief in medieval Jewish circles of the existence of witches, but it does not draw the connection, so common in the Christian world, between Satan and witches on the one hand and dybbuks on the other.[38] From the sixteenth century on,

---

[37] On demonic possession in the Christian world, see Walker, *Unclean Spirits* (above, n. 13) and Chajes, "Judgment Sweetened" (above, n. 13). See also Shulamit Shaḥar, *The Fourth Estate: A History of Women in the Middle Ages*, trans. from the Hebrew by Chaya Galai (London; New York: Methuen, 1983), index, s.v. "witchcraft," "possession"; Mary Douglas, ed., *Witchcraft: Confessions and Accusations.* London: Tavistock, 1970; Vincent Crapanzano and Vivien Garrison, eds., *Case Studies in Spirit Possession.* New York: John Wiley & Sons, 1977. The most common charge of damage to persons leveled against witches in Poland at the time was that they cast possession spells. The technical Polish term for the phenomenon is "entry of a devil" (*zadajac diabla*). The last witch trial in Poland was held as late as 1775, while the last witch trial in Switzerland took place in 1782. The accused, Anna Goldi, forty-eight years old, was executed for having signed a pact with the devil. Eighty percent of the hundred thousand people who were executed as witches between the end of the fifteenth century and the end of the eighteenth century were women.

[38] *Sefer ḥasidim*, ed. Jehuda Wistinetzki and Jakob Freimann (Frankfurt: 1923), index s.v. *kishuf* and *mekhashefot* [=witchcraft and witches]. Cf. Joshua

all surviving accounts of dybbuks in the Jewish world deal with the disembodied souls of wicked sinners. It seems that, from the point of view of the Jewish community of the sixteenth and seventeenth centuries, these disembodied souls of sinners were seen as part of the conclusive evidence of supernatural phenomena, whose existence was recruited against disconcerting new rational arguments of the early modern period, expressed in Christian and Jewish circles alike. These arguments endeavored to abandon the beliefs in the eternity of the soul and in the veracity of divine punishment after death relating to purgatory, *gehinnom* (hell), demons and transmigration of the souls. The dybbuk stories augmented the moral system of reward and punishment beyond the constraints of the visible world. They did it by demonstrating in the public arena the story of "the sin and its punishment": on account of their grave offenses, these sinners are doomed to wander restlessly after death, denied proper burial and appropriate rest in the world of the dead and subject to eternal torment and persecution. The body infiltrated by the disembodied soul is regarded as a place of repose and shelter, for as long as the soul remains within a living body, it may not be touched by the demons and destructive angels that pursue it in order to impose punishment.[39]

R. Elijah Falkon, wrote in the middle of the sixteenth century in the concluding remarks of a report on a possession that he witnessed in Safed: "And the eye that sees this writing of mine and the ear that hears it should believe with complete faith as if he has heard it from the mouth of the spirit, and should fear and be afraid and believe everything written in the Torah and in the words of the rabbis of blessed memory… and his soul will

---

Trachtenberg, *Jewish Magic and Superstition: A Study in Folk Religion.* New York: Behrman, the Jewish Book House, 1939.

[39] On torments of the spirit, see Bilu, "*Ha-dibbuk ba-yahadut*" (above, n. 8), 55–56; Yassif, *The Hebrew Folktale* (above, n. 17), 358–361, 363–370.

cleave to God."[40] Yassif argues that this possession report, as many others, should not be read as mere factual accounts pertaining to the history of spirit possession, since the writer has an explicit goal: to proselytize and strengthen the belief in God and his commandments, in a generation that has started to lose its grip on it.[41]

Spirits in the Exorcism Ceremony

In the course of exorcising a dybbuk, the participating community representatives induce the spirit to speak. Their written accounts of exorcism rituals include the dialogue conducted regarding the spirit's identity and the nature of its offense. An examination of those accounts shows that nearly all the spirits involved were of people who, during their lifetimes, had rejected the authority and discipline of the community, disturbed the religious and social order, disregarded important distinctions and breached the bounds of convention, or committed the gravest offenses against rules and norms, violating even the cardinal prohibitions – against bloodshed, incestuous or adulterous sexual unions, or idolatry – violations that are punishable by death. Prominent by their number in these accounts are instances of converts from Judaism, apostates, informers and slanderers, murderers, individuals who were hanged or drowned, necromancers, thieves, committers of incest and adultery, and suicides. The spirits tell the community representatives who engage them in conversation that they are being punished for forbidden sexual relations, for begetting *mamzerim* (children of forbidden unions), or for bloodshed or idolatry.

[40] Chajes, *Between Worlds* (n. 8 above), 148.

[41] Yassif, "*Between Worlds*" (book review) (above, n. 8), 182.

Their words imply that anyone who, during his life, disturbs the social order and causes torment to another is himself punished, tormented, and denied posthumous repose.

The moralistic lesson of these accounts was that apostates, murderers and adulterers – sinners who disturb the demarcation between holiness and impurity, norm and deviance, the community and what lies outside it – are punished by a disturbance in the demarcation between the domains of life and death. The disembodied spirit neither lives nor dies. Instead, it wanders endlessly, pursued by tormenting angels that bar it even from entering Gehenna. Beyond that moralistic tendency, however, many of those possessed by dybbuks expressed their deviance from the norm by abandoning Judaism and drawing nearer to Christianity, be it through the dybbuk's involvement in the sins of apostasy and conversion – which became surprisingly widespread – or be it through the person possessed engaging in mad, deviant conduct that showed associations with Christian rituals and groups.[42]

---

[42] For dozens of examples, see Nigal, *Sippurei dibbuk* (above, n. 11), index, s.v. *hamarat dat*, 294, and the discussion in the introduction, 31; Bilu, "*Ha-dibbuk ba-yahadut*" (above, n. 8), 548–549. On the extent of conversion among Jews in Germany and Eastern Europe, see Azriel Shoḥat, *Im ḥilufei tekufot: reshit ha-haskalah be-yahadut germaniyah* (*Beginnings of the Haskalah among German Jewry*). Jerusalem: Mossad Bialik, 1961, chap. 9, "*Hamarat ha-dat*" (Conversion), 174–197 and nn. 315–323; Benjamin Ze'ev Kedar, "*Hemshekhiyut ve-ḥiddush ba-hamarah ha-yehudit be-germaniyah shel ha-me'ah ha–18*" (Continuity and innovation in conversion from Judaism in eighteenth-century Germany), in Immanuel Etkes and Joseph Salmon, eds., *Perakim be-toledot ha-ḥevrah ha-yehudit bi-yemei ha-beinayim ve-ha-et ha-ḥadashah mukdashim le-professor ya`akov kaẓ bi-mel'oat lo shiv'im ve-ḥamesh shanah al yedei talmidav va-ḥaverav* (Chapters in the history of medieval and modern Jewish society presented by his students and colleagues to Professor Jacob Katz on his seventy-fifth birthday). Jerusalem: Magnes Press, 1980, 154–170; Jacob Goldberg, *Ha-mumarim be-mamlekhet polin*

But the ambivalent relation to the Christian world – involving both attraction and repulsion – was not the only thing spoken of by the spirits engaged in conversation by the exorcists. We also find talk of sexual promiscuity, forbidden desires, and dark deeds, of broken taboos and of incest. The stories may echo actual events or tell of genuine fears, or they may be externalizations of forbidden impulses and suppressed desires of the victim, the spirit, or the exorcist – whose task is to transform the obscure voice embodied in the spirit's noises into understandable speech. It

---

lita (Converted Jews in the Polish Commonwealth), Hebrew translation from the Polish by Tsofiyah Lasman. Jerusalem: Merkaz Zalman Shazar, 1986; Rachel Elior, ed., *Ha-ḥalom ve-shivro: ha-tenu'ah ha-shabbeta'it ve-sheluḥotehah – shabbeta'ut, meshiḥiyut, frankizm* (*The Sabbatean Movement and its Aftermath: Messianism, Sabbatianism and Frankism*), 2. Jerusalem Studies in Jewish Thought, 17. Jerusalem: Hebrew University, 2001, index, s.v. *hamarat dat* (http://jewish.huji.ac.il/publications/thought.htm). For a comprehensive study on apostasy in the Jewish community see Todd M. Endelman (ed.), *Jewish Apostasy in the Modern World.* New York and London: 1987. On apostasy in the eighteenth century see Michael Stanislavski, "Jewish Apostasy in Russia: A Tentative Typology" in *ibid.*, 189–205. On apostasy in the Hasidic community in the eighteenth and nineteenth centuries see David Assaf, "*Mumar o kadosh: masa be-ikvot Rabbi Moshe, beno shel Rabbi Shneur Zalman mi-Liady*" (Apostate or saint: a journey in the path of R. Moses, the son of R. Sheneur Zalman of Liady). *Zion* 65 (2000): 453–515. An elaboration of this article is reprinted in David Assaf, *Ne'eḥaz ba-sevach: pirkei mashber u-mevocha be-toldot ha-ḥasidut* (*Caught in the Thicket: Chapters of Crisis and Discontent in the History of Hasidism*). Jerusalem: The Zalman Shazar Center, 2006), 1–136. See index, 374: *hamarat dat* (conversion). The derogatory Hebrew words *meshumadim, kofrim, mumarim, epikorsim, mitnaẓrim* and *mitpakrim* all describe converts and reflect the pain that those who left the Jewish community caused to their relatives and acquaintances. Conversion was often used as a threat against the community in time of dispute and was explained by the community as mental illness and possession. See Assaf, *Ne'eḥaz ba-sevach*, index, 375 *maḥalot nefesh* (mental illness).

is possible, as well, that the spirit, transformed into a dybbuk, is an embodiment of social deviance that is ambivalently attractive and repulsive or that gives rise to powerful tensions between holiness and impurity, faith and apostasy, loyalty and treachery, coercion and liberty, longing and prohibition. The entry of a deceased's spirit into an ill person expresses a departure from normative limits and accepted behavior; it is the prototype for and explanation of a breach of the norm that constitute a liminal stance for the victim. A clear sign of the spirit's departure from the sick person's body is the latter's return to accepted conduct in the area of religion and within the bounds of the normative patriarchal order.

Expelling the spirit involves a ritualized, sacred dialogue, called *yiḥud* ("union") between the exorcist and the spirit being expelled. It includes adjurations, recitation of mystical "intentions" (*kavvanot*), utterance of divine names and their unification, clarification of the name, identity, and biography of the sinner being expelled, reference to his sin and punishment, along with a sense of regret and a desire to repent, and, ultimately, persuading the sinner to depart the body he has possessed. The persuasive techniques involve both carrots and sticks: promises of prayer, forgiveness and repose if he agrees, threats of excommunication and exorcism against his will, through the use of adjurations and divine names, if he refuses. The ritual concludes with the separation of the bonded entities, the spirit's return to the world of the dead, renewed demarcation of the realms and reinforcement of the boundaries between them, and an overall restoration of order. Separated from the living body, the dead spirit returns to the world of the dead; no longer possessed, the living person returns to the land of the living. Proper division again exists between life and death, holiness and impurity, the revealed and the concealed, obedience and deviance, order and defiance. The deviant breach of boundaries is healed, and the norm – grounded on separate domains, clearly distinguished categories and boundaries, and a hierarchical, obedient, order – is restored.

During the last third of the sixteenth century, R. Ḥayyim Vital (1543–1620), one of the prominent disciples of R. Isaac Luria (1534–1572), known as the Holy Ari), set forth the mystical concepts and ritualistic elements pertaining to the dybbuk. Vital's source was remarks by his teacher, R. Luria, who was well known for his spiritual insight:

> My teacher, may his memory be for a blessing, taught me a *yiḥud* to be used to remove an evil spirit, God save us. On occasion, the soul of a wicked man, whose sins are so numerous that it cannot yet enter Gehenna, may wander here and there. It may sometimes enter the body of some man or woman and subdue it; this is called "the falling sickness" [epilepsy]. By means of this *yiḥud*, his soul is improved a bit, and it leaves the person's body. And this is the procedure, as I have performed it with my own hands and have experienced it: Taking the person's arm, I place my hand on his pulse, either on the left hand or the right, for that is the site of the garment in which the soul garbs itself. I declare my intention to that soul, garbed in that pulse, that it depart from there by the force of the *yiḥud*; and while sill holding his hand at the pulse, I recite the verse "Set Thou a wicked man over him; and let an adversary [*satan*] stand at his right hand" [Ps. 109:6] both forward and backward. My intention, with all the [divine] names that emerge from the verse – both in the numerical value of each word and in their initials – is… that in this way, [the spirit] will depart. And then it speaks from within the body, [responding to] whatever you ask of it, and you command it to depart. Sometimes it is necessary to sound a shofar near his ear, intending the [divine] name *qera`*

satan ["rend Satan"]…. And know that that spirit does not come alone; rather, a satan supports him and leads him in his wanderings in this way so that his recompense for his sins may be completed. And it [the soul] may do nothing without its [the satan's] permission, for God, may He be blessed, has set [the latter] as [the former's] overseer, as is written in *Zohar*, *Parashat Bo* [41b], "A wicked person is judged by his evil impulse." And that is as Scripture states, "Set Thou a wicked man over him; and let an adversary [*satan*] stand at his right hand."… And I will set before you the formula for the *kavvanah*… and you should intend that it depart by the force of all those [divine] names. If it does not depart, repeat the aforesaid verse and again intend all the mentioned names, each time concluding by stating forcefully, "Depart, depart quickly." And know that the entire enterprise depends on your being as courageous and strong-hearted as a mighty hero, having no fear that it will stubbornly refuse to heed your words. You must also order [the spirit] not to leave via any site other than between the nail of the big toe and its flesh, so as not to injure the body in which it is situated. And you must order it, with the force of the foregoing names you intended and of excommunication and banning, not to cause any harm and not to reenter the body of any other Jew whatsoever…. And know that when it speaks, the person's body remains as still as stone, and the spirit's voice emerges from its mouth without the lips moving, in a tone as soft as that of a small child…. And know that when you ask him who he is and what is his name, he will deceive you and tell you someone else's name – either to mock you or to preclude the effectiveness of your order that it depart. It is therefore necessary that you order it, by [threat of] excommunication and banning, and by force of all the aforesaid names that you intended, that it

> not deceive you at all and that it be perfectly truthful in telling you who he is and what his name is. It is necessary as well that you perform the process in purity, [following] immersion, in sanctity, and with great intention.[43]

From the point of view of those possessed, the dybbuk may be a form of rebellion against the social coercion associated with the economic, utilitarian system for conjugal matchmaking. It may also be a rebellion against other forms of domination and coercion, both physical and psychological, imposed by the strong upon the weak; or it may be a unique opportunity for a woman to speak publicly as well as an acute expression of misery and suffering. However, the exorcists who carried out the ritual took no account of these dimensions. From their perspective, the possessed body was a battlefield on which holy names and impure forces competed for domination. They invested the expulsion process with mystical, magical, and ritual qualities touching on the realm of the dead, of adjurations, curses, and excommunication. They had been given their assignment by the representatives of the sanctified communal norm, who wanted to establish the premise that one who disturbs the order of the world, even in a minor way (such as by taking a drink without reciting the requisite blessing, dwelling in a room lacking a mezuzah, fighting with the members of his household, or expressing anger in haste), opens the door to the entry of spirits from another world. Even more, they wanted to show that one who during his life breaches the limitations imposed by the

---

[43] Ḥayyim Vital, *Sha`ar ruaḥ ha-kodesh* (Jerusalem, 1912) 36a–b. See also Ada Rapoport-Albert, *Al ma`amad ha-nashim ba-shabbeta'ut* (On the Position of Women in Sabbateanism). In Elior, *Ha-ḥalom ve-shivro* (above, n. 42), *Jerusalem Studies in Jewish Thought* 16: 147–148, 187–190 (http://jewish.huji.ac.il/publications/thought.htm).

community and deliberately commits cardinal offenses will be transformed, after his death, into a restless soul and disembodied spirit.

Conducted in a sacred public space, the exorcism ceremony in the first instance embodies a confrontation with the world of the dead and a battle between holiness and impurity – a battle fraught with intense danger and entailing a mystical struggle involving holy names and unities, sounding of rams' horns, use of Torah scrolls, fumigation and adjurations, curses and excommunication. At the second stage, in which the victory of holiness over impurity becomes clear, the ritual allows for the spirit to come in contact with the rabbi or wonder-worker who can seek atonement and forgiveness on its behalf once it has confessed its sins publicly. He can also perform for it the death-related rituals it had been denied, recite Kaddish on its behalf, and study mishnaic texts that would protect it from demons and enable it to enter Gehenna and atone there for its sins. From yet another angle, the ritual makes it possible for the spirit to make its voice heard and gain the promise of its return to repose in the domain of the dead; and it allows those who speak with it in the world of the living to raise concerns weighing on the community that may be related to what has been said by the spirit – which, after all, is graced with knowledge transcending human limitations and the boundaries of life and death. During the ceremonial dialogue, the spirit discloses concealed sins on the part of the living and the dead and uncovers dark episodes from the community's past. On occasion, it can even clarify past events and foretell future events, all in accord with information it has obtained from demons and angels in the higher worlds.

Kabbalistic Background

Scholars who investigated literary and archival reports of dybbuk exorcism narratives date the beginnings of the dybbuk's appearance as an established phenomenon in the Christian and Jewish worlds to the sixteenth century. Efforts to explain the phenomenon have looked to various religious, social, and cultural changes that occurred at the dawn of the modern era and led to a growing demonization of the world.[44] Within the Jewish historical context, however, it appears that the dybbuk can be tied to the belief in transmigration of souls, a belief that gained renewed force in the wake of the Expulsion from Spain, when the bodies of many of those who died during the Expulsion and ensuing wanderings were lost and considerable interest arose in the fate of the deceased's spirits and the revival of the souls. Having experienced the arbitrary harshness of reality, the torment of exile, and the ensuing yearning for redemption, that generation was primed to seek out more determinism in reward and punishment – a determinism that might be concealed within the hidden layers of the Torah and of the surrounding world.[45] As noted, this dualistic intellectual world was created in the wake of the Spanish Expulsion and was inspired profoundly by the material suffering of the exiles and the loss of their relatives. Following the exile of the bodies, (*galut*) they developed kabbalistic inquiry about the

---

[44] Students of early modern history have argued for a connection between the dybbuk phenomenon and the demonization of the world during the sixteenth century that occurred as a reaction to rational criticism of religious beliefs and as part of the religious struggles of the Lutheran Reformation. Exorcism of demons and dybbuks, as well as witch hunts, became caught up in Catholic religious polemics against Protestants. But Chajes notes in his doctorate (above, n. 13) that of the eight dybbuk incidents attested during the sixteenth century, seven come from a Muslim milieu.

[45] Elior, "The Doctrine of Transmigration in *Galya Raza*" (above, n. 30), 227–239.

exile of the souls (*gilgul*-transmigration). The mystical experiences of the first and second generations following the critical event that entailed new expressions of *devekut* (communion with God) and new interest in *gilgul* and dybbuk. Among the prominent writers of the time were Judah Ḥayyat, who details his grueling journey in the introduction to his *Minḥat yehudah* (1495–1498); Solomon Molḥo (1500–1532), who was born a *converso*, returned to Judaism in Portugal during the 1520s, became a kabbalist who wrote about imminent redemption, and was martyred at the stake in Mantua in November 1532; and Joseph Karo (1488–1575), the noted halakhist who was also a critically important kabbalist and author of *Maggid mesharim*, his autobiographical mystical journal.[46] Inspired by Molḥo's life and death, Karo instilled new life into the voice of the *Shekhinah* and the doctrine of transmigration. Also within this group were Karo's disciples, who immigrated with him to Safed: Solomon Alkabeẓ (1505–1584), a prolific poet and author who introduced the kabbalistic rituals associated with redeeming the *Shekhinah* from her exile; and Moses Cordovero (1522–1570), who wrote broad, systematic expositions of the conceptual world of the Kabbalah as well as autobiographical books describing his mystical experiences associated with the *Shekhinah*'s redemption. Also worthy of mention are anonymous kabbalists, such as the authors of *Galya raza* and of *Avodat ha-kodesh*, works on transmigration written in the mid-sixteenth century; and the Safed kabbalists who were active during the final third of

---

[46] On Molho and Karo see Werblowsky, *Joseph Karo* (above, n. 4), 206–233 (Chapter 10); Aaron Zeev Aescoly, *Ha-tenu`ot ha-meshichiot be-yisrael* (*Jewish Messianic Movements*) (Jerusalem: Mossad Bialik: 1987), 270–439; Rachel Elior, "*Rabbi Yosef Karo ve-Rabbi Yisra'el Besht: metamorfozah mistit, hashra'ah kabbalit, ve-hafnamah ruḥanit*" (R. Joseph Karo and R. Israel Ba'al Shem Tov: mystical metamorphosis, kabbalistic inspiration, spiritual internalization). *Tarbiz* 65 (1996): 671–709 (English trans. in *Studies in Spirituality* 17, 2007).

the sixteenth century: Isaac Luria (1534–1572) and Ḥayyim Vital (1543–1620) and their disciples and successors. They produced innovations in kabbalistic thought, establishing interrelationships between exile and redemption, *sitra aḥra* and *Shekhinah*, the revealed and concealed worlds, holiness and husk, transmigration, dybbuks, souls, angels, fiends, spirits and demons. This extensive kabbalistic oeuvre formed the intellectual backdrop for a flourishing conceptual world at whose antipodes lay *devekut* (bonding) and dybbuk – two terms, from the same Hebrew stem that share a mystical-erotic quality, embody passageways between worlds, and connect the human spirit to emissaries of the hidden worlds that infiltrate body and soul. The mystical-erotic discourse that takes place within the holy domain, involving the select few who are sufficiently meritorious, connects the human spirit to the spirit of the living God, termed *Shekhinah*, in a relationship of *devekut*. That union is accomplished through elevation of the human to the supernal world or through bonding of the human and divine spirits beyond the bounds of time and place. But when that discourse takes place within the domain of the impure, it bonds, through the dybbuk, a woman's body to a disembodied spirit from the world below – a bonding that takes place in bodies that sin or are subjected to compulsion in this world. This spiritual reality brings humanity into contact with two opposing worlds: the divine realm, the source of life, holiness, redemption, eternal life, and hope, entailing bonding with the *Shekhinah* and referred to as "the world of speech" (*olam ha-dibbur*) or "higher speech" (*dibbur elyon*); and the world of the husk, the *sitra aḥra*, impurity, exile, and death – the world associated with the dybbuk, which speaks as an evil spirit from the world of the dead, the lower world.[47] Speech of the *Shekhinah*, bonding

---

[47] On bonding (*devekut*) with the "Shekhinah, the world of speech," see Gershom Scholem, "Devekut or Communion with God" in id. *The Messianic Idea in Judaism*, (New York: Schocken 1971), 228–250; Werblowsky, *Joseph Karo*

with the *Shekhinah*, revelation of a *maggid* (an embodiment of union with the *Shekhinah*), and the presence of a divine voice within a human body were attributed to the greatest of the kabbalists and Hasidic masters. Angelic mentors and divine voices speaking through the mouth of an eminent individual who had attained a state of *devekut* with the *Shekhinah* are recorded in the writings of Joseph Karo, Moses Cordovero, Isaac Luria, Ḥayyim Vital, Isaiah Horowitz, Moses Ḥayyim Luzzatto, Israel Ba`al Shem Tov, Dov Ber – the Maggid of Mezritch, Isaac ha-Levi Horowitz – the Seer of Lublin, Yeḥiel Mikhel – the Maggid of Zolochov, and Isaac Safrin of Komorno, author of *Megillat Setarim*.

This symbolic, mystical, and ritual contact with the personified, abstract, liturgical, and textual representatives of both holiness and impurity exercised a substantial effect on the communities in which it took place. Over the years it became internalized, turning into models of identity and subjects of writing, interpretation, and study. Holiness was represented by the *Shekhinah*, angels, sparks, letters, *maggidim*, souls, holy spirits, revelation of the prophet Elijah, and the Messiah. Impurity was represented by the *sitra aḥra*, Sama'el, Satan, the angel of death, demons, evil spirits, the spirits of the dead, dybbuks, and husks. This complex of ideas strengthened a worldview that recognized contact with the concealed realm

---

(above, n. 4), 206–233 (Chapter 10); Rachel Elior, "*Rabbi Yosef Karo*" (above, n. 46); Rivka Schatz-Uffenheimer, *Hasidism as Mysticism: Quietistic Elements in Eighteenth Century Hasidic Thought*, trans. from the Hebrew by Jonathan Chipman (Princeton, NJ: Princeton Univ. Press; Jerusalem: Magnes Press, 1993, 204–214; Laurence Fine, "Benevolent Spirit Possession in Sixteenth-Century Safed," in Goldish, ed., *Spirit Possession* (above, n. 8), 101–123. On the relationship between dybbuk and *devekut*, see Zvi Mark, *Mistikah ve-shiga`on bi-yeẓirat Rabbi Naḥman mi-Braslov* (*Mysticism and Madness in the Work of R. Nahman of Bratslav*). Jerusalem and Tel Aviv: Shalom Hartman Institute and Am Oved, 2003; Bilu, "Dybbuk and Maggid" (above, n. 8).

and interpreted the revealed in its light.[48] The inspiration brought about by *devekut* and by contact with the realm of the holy and the source of eternal life shared a common premise with the madness associated with the dybbuk and with contact with the impure realm and with death: both presumed that there existed linkages to hidden worlds and that a person, his soul, and his spirit were subject to influence or infiltration by some entity beyond his control, emanating from outside his consciousness and from beyond the range of the revealed world. However, it should be noted that while communion with God (*devekut*) and the articulation of divine voices through a human throat as angelic mentors (a *maggid*) or divine speech (*dibbur shekhinah*) was reserved for holy men alone, mandatory union with spirits from the world of the dead (*dybbuk*) and articulation of their voices through human voices (evil spirit) was confined mainly to women.

The writings of the sixteenth-century kabbalists afford extensive consideration to *devekut* and to illumination flowing from the higher worlds. They also consider transmigration, dybbuks, and possession by forces from the lower world. Exhaustive definitions of the phenomenon can be found in *Maggid mesharim* – devoted to the words of the angel/*maggid* who speaks from Joseph's Karo's throat – and in *Or yakar* by Moses Cordovero, which included "*Shemu`ah be-inyan ha-gilgul*" (a report of transmigration).[49] The subject is treated as well in Ḥayyim Vital's *Sefer ha-gilgulim* (Book of transmigrations), *Sha`ar ha-gilgulim (Gate of*

---

[48] On the significance of this conceptual world, see Gershom Scholem, *Sabbatai Sevi* (above, n. 3), 1–81. Werblowsky, *Joseph Karo* (above, n. 3), "Intellectual Life in Safed," 50–89; On kabbalistic groups and internalization and vitalization of the kabbalistic myth see Rachel Elior, *The Mystical Origins of Hasidism*, trans. from the Hebrew by Shalom Carmy and Connie Webber (Oxford: The Littman Library of Jewish Civilization, 2006), 27–40.

[49] Moses Cordovero, *Or yakar*, vol. 21 (Jerusalem, 1991), 79.

transmigrations), and *Sefer ha-ḥezyonot* (Book of Dreams. The archetypal model for dybbuk exorcism is *Ma`aseh ha-ruaḥ (A Tale of a spirit)*, which served as Vital's guiding text and is quoted at the beginning of *Sha`ar ha-gilgulim.*[50] Other texts by kabbalists of the period of the Expulsion and by the Safed kabbalists also consider the matter. In all of these works, consideration of the manifestations of the holy spirit in association with *devekut* is accompanied by precise definitions of evil spirits and dybbuks, their various appearances, and the proper ways to expel them.

Lurianic hagiography, widespread in the writings of the Ari's disciples Ḥayyim Vital, Jacob Ẓemaḥ, and Me'ir Poppers, was published during the seventeenth century in such works as *Ta`alumot ḥokhmah* (Mysteries of Wisdom) (Basel, 1629) and, later, in *Shivḥei ha-Ari* Phrases of Luria) (Ostrog 1794) and *Toledot ha-Ari* (Life of Luria) (Konstantinopol 1720).[51] That literature, attesting to the Ari's relationship to the world of souls, contributed to the spread of the belief in disembodied spirits and restless souls unable to find their repose; it even influenced the standard models for

---

[50] Ḥayyim Vital, *Sha`ar ha-gilgulim* (Jerusalem 1912) 1a; cf. id., *Sha`ar ruaḥ ha-kodesh* (Jerusalem 1863) 34a. The earliest documented dybbuk exorcism was conducted by R. Joseph Karo in 1545 in the Galilee; the account pertaining to an epileptic young boy infiltrated by a spirit, appears in R. Judah Halivah's book in a ms. of *Zofnat paneaḥ*. Karo threatens the spirit with excommunication and punishment in order to make him speak and reveal his identity. The curative procedure included threats, dialogue, incantations and prayers. See Moshe Idel, "*Iyyunim be-shitat ba`al sefer ha-meshiv*" [Inquires into the method of the author of Sefer ha-meshiv], *Sefunot* 2 (NS) (17) (1983), 2. 224. Cf. Werblowsky, *Joseph Karo*, (n. 3 above), 236f.

[51] See Gershom Scholem, "*Le-toledot ha-mekubbal Rabbi ya`aqov Ẓemaḥ u-fe'ulato ha-sifrutit*" [On the life and literary activities of the kabbalist R. Jacob Ẓemaḥ], *Kiryat Sefer* 15 (1950): 185–194; Benayahu, *Sefer toledot ha-ari* (above, n. 4), 290–306.

healing dybbuk cases and expelling evil spirits. Works published in the seventeenth and eighteenth centuries provided convincing evidence of supernatural appearances such as evil spirits, spirits of the deceased, wandering souls, dangerous demons, and threatening witches, that explain the side-by-side coexistence of the world of the dead with the world of the living and the status of its occupants in relation to their moral qualities during their terrestrial live. Such works were Menasseh ben Israel, *Nishmat ḥayyim* (The Spirit of Life) (Amsterdam 1652), *Yosef omeẓ* (Added Courage) (Frankfurt, 1723), composed in the early seventeenth century and published by Joseph Yospa Hahn, the *shamash* of the Worms community; *Yesod yosef* (Joseph's Foundation) (Shklov 1785), written in 1679 by Joseph Yoska ben Judah of Dubnow; and *Kav ha-yashar* (Frankfurt a/M, 1705), written by his student, Ẓevi Hirsch Koidonover, and printed dozens of times throughout the eighteenth century. For example, a sinner's restless soul may be connected at various stages to the menace that hovers over life or to various terrestrial manifestations of mental illness, construed as a deceased's spirit bonding to a living body. Ẓevi Hirsch Koidonover cites an illustration of this concept by the Ari:

> Now in this chapter, I will write briefly about the punishment for a soul impaired by a person in this world. Know that the air of the world's space is filled with souls of people who cannot yet come to their place of repose, as attested by the disciples of the Ari, of blessed memory, who would say to them: "Know that the air of the world and its space are filled with driven souls not yet able to attain repose." And once the Ari of blessed memory went to study Torah in the fields and he himself saw all the trees filled

with innumerable souls; and, indeed, there were above the field and above the water as well several myriads of souls.[52]

In works such as *Sefer ha-ḥezyonot* (Book of Dreams), *Shivḥei ha-ari* (In Praise of R. Isaac Luria), *Sha'ar ha-gilgulim* (Gate of Transmigrations), *Kav ha-yashar*, *Iggeret ha-kodesh* (The Holy Epistle) by Israel Ba'al Shem Tov (1781), *Shivḥei ha-besht* (In Praise of the Ba'al Shem Tov) (1815), and the letters of Moses Ḥayyim Luzzatto (1937), this world of driven souls is depicted as the background for the redemptive activity in the supernal worlds of the mystical hero whose praises are being told. The heroes make their way to that world through intention and unification formulas (*kavvanot* and *yiḥudim*) and remain there in *devekut*, exercising curative force in this world, from which they expel dybbuks with the force of holy names, adjurations, unifications, fumigations, and excommunications.

Exorcism and Unification: Between Expulsion of the Dybbuk and the Wedding Ceremony

The documents that have come down to us suggest that the dybbuk exorcists tended to be rabbis, kabbalists, "masters of the Name" (*ba`alei shem*) or *ẓaddikim* (lit., "righteous ones"; in context, Hasidic leaders and wonder-workers) who could draw inferences from physical ailments to illnesses of the soul and conversely. They were prepared to participate in the healing of patients through a public ritual procedure that treats body and soul as a part of the socio-communal structure and interweaves the struggle between holiness and impurity with that between norm and

[52] *Kav ha-yashar*. Vilna: 1927, chapter 5, 16–1.

deviance. Administration of the process required expertise in the holy Names and the interrelationships between revealed and concealed, all connected with the unification formulas set forth in the kabbalistic literature. Among these exorcists were Joseph Karo, Ḥayyim Vital, Israel Ba`al Shem Tov, Israel of Koznitz, and other Hasidic *ẓaddikim*.

The exorcism ceremony proceeded on several planes simultaneously. It had a therapeutic aspect, related to the movement between lucidity and madness as connected to the world of the living and the world of the dead, but it also was a highly perilous mystical-magical ritual. It entailed confrontation between the purifying world of the living and the contaminating world of the dead, a struggle between the worlds of sanctity and impurity, between order and chaos, normal and abnormal, and life and death. The body possessed by the dybbuk became the arena in which the battle between the holy names and the forces of impurity was staged. The battle itself was played out as the triumph of the holy language of names, prayers, adjurations and unification formulas over the impure language of the dead heard through threats and curses and chaotic speech from the dybbuk's mouth; and as the victory of established adjurations and excommunication formulas over the unpredictable speech rising up from the spirit's mouth.[53] The dybbuk mediates between the two worlds, for its breaching of norms is construed as breaching the boundaries between life

---

[53] On the magical language of unification formulas and holy Names, see Rachel Elior, *Jewish Mysticism: The Infinite Expression of Freedom,* trans. from the Hebrew by Yudith Nave and Arthur B. Millman. Oxford: The Littman Library of Jewish Civilization, 2007, 90–98; id., "Mysticism, Magic and Angelology: The Perception of Angels in Hekhalot Literature," *Jewish Studies Quarterly* (Tübingen) 1, 1 (1993–1994): 5–53; Rebecca M. Lesses, *Ritual Practice to Gain Power: Angels, Incantations, and Revelation in Early Jewish Mysticism.* Harrisburg, PA: Trinity Press, 63–101.

and death, between purity and impurity, and between this world and the world to come.

Because the dramatic ceremony opened a passageway between worlds, it entailed the dangers of contact with the world of the dead. To combat chaos and the fear of death, it was necessary to follow a strict ritual order, entailing models, paradigms, and numbers associated with purity and impurity. It was also necessary to use excommunications and adjurations to fortify the boundaries between holiness and impurity. The ritual was conducted in the synagogue, where a prayer quorum of ten men (a *minyan*) gathered after having purified themselves through fasting and immersion. They were dressed in shrouds (the *kittel,* a white garment also worn on the Day of Atonement), prayer shawls, and phylacteries. The Ark was opened, seven ram's horns were sounded simultaneously, seven Torah scrolls were removed from the Ark, seven black candles were lit, a black curtain was placed over the Ark, incense was burned, and the adjurations, curses, and excommunications that threaten demons and evil spirits were recited. In unison, the entire congregation repeated the curses, the excommunication formula, and a poem considered to be an anti-demonic formula (Psalm 91 or an old prayer attested in *hekhalot* literature known as *Aleinu le-shabeaḥ*; the latter is also routinely used in daily worship). They then recited seven different combinations of the forty-two-letter divine name, which incorporate the phrase *kera' satan* ("rend Satan").[54] The exorcism

[54] On dybbuk exorcism ceremonies, see Nigal, *Sippurei dibbuk* (above, n. 11), 77–85, 96–105, 132–134, 154–172, and index s.v. *megareshim*, 295. On the forty–two-letter name, see Ephraim E. Urbach, *The Sages: Their Concepts and Beliefs*, trans. from the Hebrew by Israel Abrahams (Jerusalem: Magnes Press, 1987), Chap. VII ("The Power of the Divine Name"), 130–131. Cf. the account of the exorcism in S. An-sky's play *Between Two Worlds (The Dybbuk)*, trans. Joachim Neugroschel, in *The Dybbuk and the Yiddish Imagination: A Haunted Reader*, ed. and trans. from the Yiddish by Joachim Neugroschel. Syracuse, NY: Syracuse University Press,

ceremony is focused on the battle between sanctity and impurity, between holy names and voices from the world of the dead, between representatives of the world of the living, who sanctify and purify themselves, and the unseen emissary of the world of the dead, who defiles and disrupts order.

I suggested earlier a linkage between the dybbuk's entry and the possessed woman's removal from the circle of social expectations related to matchmaking, marriage, and sexual relations. (Among other things, entry of the dybbuk precludes consummation of a marriage because the body possessed by the dybbuk carries the impurity associated with the dead.) In light of that premise, it seems reasonable to examine the interrelationship between two rites of passage related to the body and its cultural appropriation: the marriage ceremony and the ceremony for exorcising a dybbuk. Both ceremonies pertain to the stem *d-b-k* and entail changes in the limits of entry and exit, contain elements of consent and coercion, and proceed on symbolic, ritual, and social planes.

In analyzing the dybbuk exorcism ceremony as it pertains to the situation most often described in the narratives – a deceased male spirit having infiltrated a female body – we find, on several interpretive levels, a sort of photographic negative of the wedding ceremony, in which male and female are united (after the phrasing in Genesis 2:24: *ve-davak be-ishto,* "he shall cling to his wife"). Both are rites of passage, that is, ceremonies that accompany a person at a time of significant biological, spiritual, or social change and help one overcome the hardships of moving from one

---

2000, 3–52.) Cf. S. An-sky, *The Dybbuk and Other Writings,* edited by David G. Roskies, trans. Golda Werman. New Haven: Yale University Press, 2002.

As part of the exorcism ceremony seven ram's horns are sounded, seven black candles are lit, and the ark is covered with a black curtain (id., 47–48). On the exorcism's role in strengthening the cultural values of the community, see Bilu, "*Ha-dibbuk ba-yahadut*" (above, n. 8).

social role and one physical and mental status to another. These rites confirm substantive changes in the boundaries between life and death that are understood as critical situations requiring special ritual attention.

The wedding ceremony, which takes place in the synagogue in the presence of a *minyan*, affords a sacred quality, under the community's auspices, to the passage of two people from being single individuals to being a couple. The community expresses praise for the continuity, union, and fertility implicit in their becoming "one flesh" (Gen. 2:24). Analogously, the ceremony for exorcising a dybbuk, which likewise takes place in the synagogue, in the presence of a *minyan*, affords a ceremonial quality to the passage from a state of coerced coupling to one of separation. The coerced coupling – the clinging of a spirit of a dead person to a living body – is regarded as deviation from the norm; the ceremony restores the norm that separates coercer from coerced. It does so by expelling the dead spirit and freeing the living body from the dybbuk's clutch, thereby dissolving the compelled sexual union and signifying the possibility of normal continuity and formation of life.

What occurs during the exorcism ceremony is a sworn separation between spirit and body, between the spirit of a dead man and the body of a living/dead woman on whom he has forced himself, coercing her into submission and breaching her integrity. In contrast, the marriage ceremony comprises a sworn union of body with body, signified by the covenant between bride and groom. That covenant involves a mutual undertaking and voluntary agreement on the part of the couple to breach their bodily bounds through *devekut* and union. In both ceremonies, the rabbi, representing the community, carries out the process that establishes coupling and union or expulsion and separation, as the case may be. In both ceremonies he does so in a fixed ritual manner agreed upon in advance, in accord with a sanctified, written text – the *ketubbah* (marriage contract) that establishes a covenant between two people, or the bill of excommunication that establishes expulsion. The exorcism ceremony includes adjurations, unification formulas, curses, and excommunications; they entail use of sacred names, oaths, and threats to restore the preexisting boundaries and order.[55] The wedding ceremony includes *ketubbah* and blessings, canopy and bride acquisition; they constitute sanctification of a breach of boundaries (between the two individuals) bound to a sacred oath and to promises of blessings related to the establishment of a new order. During the wedding ceremony, the ring that adorns the bride's finger symbolizes the transition from individual to member of a couple. Analogously, the amulet tied to the victim's body during the exorcism symbolizes completion of the expulsion rite and the transition from member of a coerced couple to free individual.[56] In both ceremonies, care is taken to call out the names of the protagonists, for names and the identities of their bearers are of substantive importance, preconditions on the one hand to entering the covenant and changing the bride's name and, on the other, to expelling the spirit that depends on the manifestation of a name. Only after the sprit discloses his name does he deliver himself into the hands of the *ba`al shem* or the rabbi, who uncovers his identity and is then able to expel him. In both ceremonies, there are preconditions to the process that effectuates the change: the spirit places conditions on his yielding the body,[57] just as the members of the couple or their agents

[55] For examples in which the spirit is compelled to swear and even to sign a guarantee that he will depart, see Nigal, *Sippurei dibbuk* (above, n. 11), 181.

[56] Id., 54, 206, 231.

[57] On the "conditions" imposed by the spirit – including the recitation of Kaddish on his behalf, lighting candles in his memory, endowing a dinner for impoverished scholars, annulling excommunications, and studying *mishnayyot* for the benefit of his soul – see Nigal, id., 143–144, 179, 181, 189, 210–221; Bilu, "*Ha-dibbuk ba-yahadut*" (above, n. 8), 551.

establish conditions for the marriage. As noted, both ceremonies are rites of passage that confirm a substantive change in the boundaries between life and death and are understood as critical situations needing special ritual attention on the part of the participants: immersion, purification, abstinence, and sanctification, all in advance of the ceremony.[58] The traditional order in some parts of the Ashkenazi world requires the participants to wear white burial shrouds.[59] Both rituals take place in the synagogue, under a prayer shawl or canopy, by the light of black candles in the case of an exorcism or white candles in the case of a wedding. Each reflects the obverse of the other: the wedding ceremony pertains to the establishment of new life within society, affording society's protection and

---

[58] On the purification and abstinence practices engaged in before the exorcism ceremony, see Nigal, id., 43.

[59] On the preparation of burial shrouds for the bride, see *Kehal ḥasidim* (above, n. 31), 108. On shrouds at nuptials, see Corinne Ze'evi-Weill, *Ma`arekhet takhriḥim mei-alzas* [A set of shrouds from Alsace], in *Yahadut alzas: kehillah kafrit bein masoret le-emanẓipaẓiyah* [The Jews of Alsace: a rural community between tradition and emancipation], exhibition catalog ed. by Ester Muchawsky-Schnapper, (Israel Museum, 1991), 34–54 (also in French as *Les Juifs d'Alsace: village, tradition, émancipation*). Ze'evi-Weill writes: "It was the practice to wear specific components of the set of shrouds at various life-cycle events… decorated parts were worn at festive events, first among them the wedding day, when they were worn under the festive garments…. In religious circles of eastern European origin, it is still the practice to dress the groom, as he is led to the wedding canopy, in a *kittel* (white robe, also a burial shroud), placing it above his shirt or under his coat. Other communities also have the custom of somehow connecting shrouds and wedding clothes" (44). On Ashkenazi custom linking weddings and mourning, see Samuel Glick, *Or nagah aleihem: ha-zikah she-bein minhegei nisu'in le-minhegei avelut be-masoret yisra'el* [*Light Has Dawned: the connection between wedding customs and mourning customs in Jewish tradition*] (Efrat: Keren Ori, 1997); on the specific connection between shrouds and weddings, see id., 127–143.

blessing to a sacred covenant of unity, purity, *devekut* and coupling, whose purpose is continuity and fertility; the exorcism ceremony pertains to a willful breach of boundaries, involving forced, forbidden coupling that challenges the limitations imposed by society. The dybbuk represents banishment, impurity, death, and destruction; and society strives to expel and excommunicate it. Conjugal union takes place in private, willingly and consensually, following a public wedding ceremony; in contrast, expulsion of the dybbuk involves public disclosure of sins performed in private, arbitrarily and violently. The dybbuk uses an illness to dramatize the coercive conquest of a body by an infiltrating foreign entity, implicitly referring to the compulsion that took place secretly, in the private domain; its exorcism makes those events public. These contrasts exist both on the plane of the idea itself and on the plane of its symbolic representation. We find, in the case of the wedding, completeness, entry into a covenant, purification, blessing, and the mystery of *devekut* (fasting, sanctification, immersion, white garments, the seven wedding blessings, white candles), all of which establish the continuity of life and fertility. In the case of the exorcism, we find, in contrast, licentiousness, arbitrariness, violence, coercion, compulsion, and public activity of the dybbuk, which emerges from the world of the dead (black garments, black candles, curses, and excommunication) – the domain of cardinal sins associated with destruction.

The two ceremonies share several points of contact along the border between life and death. The right of passage from a state of virginity and a degree of individual freedom to one of conjugal subservience, involving a loss of liberty and a not insignificant element of coercion, was a risky time of exposure to trouble. It brought into focus the tensions between a coerced norm and social regulation on the one hand and, on the other, the implicit possibility of rebellion. It also raised the fears and tensions associated with states of transition, crisis, and change – states that link past with future and fertility with destruction. As noted earlier, many of the possession stories and exorcism reports are directly connected to the wedding, a transitory stage in life. It is evident from various aspects of the tradition that the Jewish ritual life cycle – circumcision, bar mitzvah, wedding, – was regarded as perpetually threatened by injury or death and vulnerable to harm by supernatural forces. The wedding ceremony is associated in Jewish tradition with the wearing of shrouds on the one hand and the hope for new life on the other; it thus illustrates the danger of death and catastrophe implicit in a situation whose purpose is to create a framework for continuing and renewing life but whose essence is tied to the premise that human beings live simultaneously in different worlds, revealed and concealed, that participate in the struggle between fertility and destruction.

Numerous written traditions and ritual customs allude to the liminal significance of rites of passage and the poles of life and death between which the hidden drama, beyond the overt ceremony, is played out. Notable among these customs are the tradition of the "dance of death" at a wedding, which offers an opportunity to mingle the world of the dead with the world of the living and the past with the future; the appearance of the angel of death at a wedding in the form of a beggar; the verse "Charity saves from death" uttered by the beggars, which affords bride and groom the opportunity to escape death by observing the commandment and alludes to the tension and danger inherent in the ritual; pre-marriage visits to the graves of deceased relatives who cannot take part in the ceremony; and stories of the "serpent on the wedding night," which connect death and marriage – all of these were widespread within Jewish culture.[60]

---

[60] On the dance of death at a wedding, see *The Memoirs of Glückel of Hameln*, trans. from the Yiddish with notes by Marvin Lowenthal; new introd. by Robert S. Rosen. New York: Schocken Books, 1977 (orig. published New York and London:

Between Two Worlds (The Dybbuk) – S. An-sky

The wedding ceremony and dybbuk exorcism ceremony, as photographic negative images of each other, are presented in S. An-sky's famous play *Between Two Worlds (The Dybbuk)*. The play, written in Yiddish between 1912 and 1917, appeared in a Hebrew translation by Ḥayyim Naḥman Bialik in the first issue of *Ha-tekufah* (Tevet–Adar 5678 1917–1918). The earliest English translation was published in New York in 1926. In writing the play, which depicts Jewish life in eastern European communities during

---

Harper & Bros. 1932), 99. A Hebrew translator of the memoir comments that "the dance of death was practiced by Christians in their churches from the fourteenth century and on; it had an allegorical aspect demonstrating the power of death over life. Especially popular was the painting of the dance of death in the Marienkirche at Lübeck, and the Jews, drawn to their neighbors' customs, adopted this custom as well" (*Zikhronot glikel* [Glückel's memoirs], Hebrew trans. by Alexander Ziskind Rabinowitz. Tel Aviv: Dvir, 1929, 63). On the dance of death in medieval European culture, see James M. Clark, *Dance of Death by Hans Holbein.* London: Phaidon Press, 1947. On the beggars' dance in relation to weddings, see Avidav Lipsker, "*Ha-kallah ve-shive`at ha-kabẓanim – li-she'elat mekorotav shel sippur ha-misgeret shel ma`aseh me-ha–7 betlers*" [The bride and the seven beggars – on the sources of the frame story of the seven beggars], *Jerusalem Studies in Jewish Folklore*, 13–14 (1992): 229–248; Glick, *Or nagah aleihem* (above, n. 59), 184–185. Cf. throughout An-sky's play, next considered. The dance of death was mounted in the Warsaw production of *The Dybbuk* as a dramatic interpretation not included in the text of the play; for a film of the production, see the Hebrew University Spielberg Film Archive. On the linkage in folktales between weddings and death, see also Galit Ḥazzan-Rokem, "*Ha-naḥash be-leil ha-kelulot: he'arah semiyotit la-shitah ha-mashvah be-ḥeker ha-sippur ha-amami*" (The serpent on the wedding night: a semiotic note on the comparative method in the study of folktales). *Bikkoret u-parshanut* 30 (Elul 5754 [1994]): 25–40. On the story of R. Reuben's bride and the angel of death, see the index entry for it in Yassif, *The Hebrew Folktale* (above, n. 17).

the eighteenth and nineteenth centuries, An-sky (a pseudonym for Solomon Zanvil Rappoport, 1863–1920) relied not only on Jewish sources of various sorts but also on ethnographic and folkloric material. His Jewish sources included *Sippur dibbuk*, a dybbuk narrative told by the rabbi of Chelmnik in 1748 (Warsaw, 1908);[61] the booklet *Ma`asiyah nora'ah* (Warsaw, 1908);[62] the tales of R. Naḥman of Bratslav on king and emperor, burgher and peon (Kopyst? 1815); the tales of *Kehal ḥasidim* (Lemberg 1825); and *Sippur ha-betulah mi-ludomir* (The Story of the Maid of Ludomir) (St. Petersburg 1910)[63] The ethnographic and folkloric material had been

---

[61] See Nigal, *Sippurei dibbuk* (above, n. 11), 116–124. Cf. Bilu, *Ha-dibbuk ba-yahadut* (above, n. 8), n. 27.

[62] Nigal, id., 146–162.

[63] On the tale of the woman, endowed with extraordinary spiritual qualities and electing a life of isolation and asceticism, who is nevertheless married off against her will so that she is brought back within the accepted order, see Mordecai Bieber, "*Ha-almah mi-ludomir*" [The Maid of Ludomir], *Reshumot* (NS) 2 (1946): 69–76. Bieber there refers to a note by "S.A.G." (Sh.A. Horodecky) on the Maid of Ludomir, published in Russian in 1910 in *Yevreskaya Starina*. This appears to be the earliest written documentation of the episode, and the time of its publication allows for the possibility that An-sky was influence by this tradition, among others, as he wrote *The Dybbuk*. In Jochanan Twersky, *Ha-betulah mi-ludomir* (The Maid of Ludomir), Tel Aviv, 1949, the physician concludes by saying "You know, despite all the misfortunes in her life and the struggles she encountered along the way, it seems to me that her life was not merely a collection of random events. For many generations, the Jewish woman lacked a voice. She sought to give her that voice." See also Rapoport-Albert, "On Women in Hasidism, S.A. Horodecky and the Maid of Ludmir Tradition" (above, n. 5). A similar story pertaining to subjugation of exceptional women who rebelled against the norms of the patriarchal society when they wanted to integrate in the scholarly and spiritual circles is told about Aidel Rokeach, the beloved daughter of Rabbi Shalom of Belz (1783–1855). A gifted woman, she aspired to officiate as a Zaddik in the first half of the nineteenth century in Brody while challenging the spiritual leadership of her brother

gathered by the first ethnographic expedition sponsored by Baron Ginzburg, sent to Volhynia and Podolia in 1912–1914. The expedition, in which An-sky participated, set out to conduct a comprehensive study of the regions known as "The Pale of Settlement" on behalf of the Jewish Society for the Study of Folklore and Ethnography, based in St. Petersburg.[64]

It is evident that the wedding ceremony in An-sky's play serves as the epicenter for a clash between social norm (matchmaking) and individual

---

Joshua. She was labeled by her criticized brother as mentally ill and as possessed by a dybbuk, and he was the one who performed the ritual of the exorcism. See: Dov Sadan, *Me-mehoz ha-yaldut* (From the district of my childhood). Tel Aviv: 1981, 256–264; Yoram Bilu, "Dybbuk Possession and Mechanism of Internalization and Externalization: A Case Study." In *Projection, Identification, Projective Identification,* edited by Joseph Sandler, 163–178. Madison, Connecticut: 1987.

[64] See Samuel Werses, "'*Bein shenei olamot (ha-dibbuk)*' *le-S. An-sky be-gilgulav ha-tekstualiyim*" (An-sky's *Between Two Worlds [The Dybbuk]* in its textual incarnations). *Ha-sifrut* 3–4 (35–36) (1986): 154–194; *Back to the Shtetl: An-sky and the Jewish Ethnographic Expedition, 1912–1914*, from the collections of the State Ethnographic Museum (St. Petersburg), exhibition catalogue, ed. Rivka Gonen, Israel Museum: 1994. The folklore scholar Eli Yassif noted that "the play *Between Two Worlds*" was published in 1917. It became the most successful Jewish play of all time, known by a different title, "The Dybbuk." The play was based on the materials he collected between 1911 and 1914 in the ethnographic expedition in the Pale of Settlement, the major Jewish settlement in nineteenth-century Russia-Poland. Together with many contemporaries, An-sky saw in "The Dybbuk" "an authentic expression of the Jewish folk zeitgeist" (Yassif, 2006, n. 8 above, 179). Zalman Shazar, who was raised in an eastern European Hasidic family and studied the history of the sixteenth-century Safed kabbalists and their Hasidic successors in Europe, wrote about the play eighty years ago: "This folkloric material was not made up or invented; it was lived for hundreds of years in Poland and other places where Hasidism prevailed. It is as if all of them come together as a living body not yet touched by the hand of art." "*Mishpat 'ha-dibbuk'*" (The dybbuk trial), Tel Aviv, 1926, 37; quoted in Werses, id., 157.

desire (unfulfilled love); it is a setting fated for trouble. The trouble is realized at the end of the second act: Leah, the bride, rebels against the arranged marriage and rejects her bridegroom, crying out "You are not my bridegroom." Nakhman, the groom's father, declares "She's lost her mind," and the Messenger ends the act with the dramatic pronouncement that "A dead soul has entered the body of the bride: a dybbuk." An-sky was quite clear about his intention: "My play, needless to say, is a realistic drama about mystics.... Throughout the play there is a battle between the individual and the collective – more precisely, between the individual's striving for happiness and the survival of the nation. Khónon and Leah struggle for their personal happiness, while the tzaddik's only worry is that 'a living branch will wither on the eternal tree of Israel. Which side is right?'"[65]

The play powerfully and dramatically depicts the clash between the powerful social norm of arranged marriage and the powerless striving for personal choice and individual freedom. As the product of the patriarchal family's social endeavors, the arranged marriage clearly expresses the traditional, authoritative concept that regulates the lives of the community's members in accord with a system of deliberate and utilitarian interconnections and obligations. The principle of personal choice sets itself against this order by breaching norms related to body or mind or by means of a dybbuk, the external manifestation of internalized feelings. It is the latter that is so powerfully dramatized in An-sky's play.

An-sky uses the dybbuk to express the profound inner connection between Leah and Khónon, two souls deeply in love who had been promised to each other by their fathers through solemn agreement even

---

[65] Letter of An-sky to Ḥayyim Zhitlovsky, written in 1920 and published in *Literarishe Bletter* 11 (July 1924): 2. English translation by Joachim Neugroschel, in id., *The Dybbuk and the Yiddish Imagination* (above, n. 54), 1.

before they were born and who had lived their lives in inner closeness to each other. Their external connection, however, was arbitrarily dissolved by Leah's father, who reneged on his promise after Khónon's father died. Khónon, denied fulfillment of his love, devoted himself to involvement in practical Kabbalah, inspired by the ancient story about "the four who entered the orchard," (Hagigah 14b)[66] and died. Leah's father chose another bridegroom for her, Menashe, but the match was arranged by the two fathers through economic and financial negotiations and imposed on Leah against her will. The dissolution of the union between Leah and Khónon on the mystical level – related to the holy world in its terrestrial embodiment (oath and solemn agreement, covenant between two lovers, voluntary betrothal, heavenly matchmaking) – calls forth the dybbuk, which unites the soul of the deceased Khónon with Leah. He thereby annuls her coerced betrothal to Menashe, with whose soul hers is not joined in the world of the living, through the union that takes place in the world of the dead, connecting the hidden and the revealed. Whether it be called dybbuk, madness, the "abnormal," or the supernatural, the unity of the living Leah with her deceased beloved Khónon or her "possession" by him, the phenomenon liberates Leah from union with Menashe, her living bridegroom. It suffuses the bride's body and soul and disrupts the normative order that the community would reinforce through the anticipated wedding.

---

[66] See G. Scholem, *Major Trends in Jewish Mysticism*, New York: Schocken 1941, 52–53; idem., *Jewish Gnosticism, Merkabah Mysticism, and Talmudic Tradition*, New York: The Jewish Theological Seminary, 1960, 14–19; Rachel Elior, *The Three Temples: On the Emergence of Jewish Mysticism*, trans. from the Hebrew by David Louvish. Oxford; Portland, OR: Littman Library of Jewish Civilization, 2004, 232–265.

The community fails in its effort at ritual exorcism of the dybbuk. In the first instance, the ritual is based on linking the world of the dead to the world of the living and then, in its second phase, on undoing the tie between concealed and revealed and attempting to reestablish the breached dichotomy between life and death. But the community is frustrated in its desire to restore the norm. When the bride could not live up to the community's imposed expectations, she fled to the supernatural or abnormal realm. The unwanted match imposed on her would have established an external connection meant to replace her inner connection to her beloved, which had been arbitrarily dissolved by circumstance. But instead of submitting to that arrangement, the mad bride and dead groom recover their inner connection in a way that transfers them beyond the limits of time and space. In the traditional scheme, as noted, the supernatural and abnormal worlds existed just outside the boundaries of this world. It appears that when an individual, whether man or woman, could not meet conventionally imposed expectations or respond to the social dynamic associated with the various aspects of arranged marriages, his soul might call upon the dybbuk in rebellion against social coercion. One afflicted by a dybbuk is freed from the terrestrial world's dominion by force of the concealed world that adjoins the liminal domain between life and death, lucidity and madness, conjugal union and dybbuk.[67] As an

---

[67] S.Y. Agnon's well known story "*Sippur pashut*" (A simple story) depicts the development of this sort of madness in Hershel, who is subjected to an unwanted match and forbidden to marry his beloved. Agnon's famous story "Tehillah" tells of a bride, Tehillah's daughter, who flees to a convent on the eve of her wedding: "And when did she flee [and enter the convent and convert]? At the time she was to be led to the wedding canopy." S.Y. Agnon, *Ad henah* (above, n. 4), 189. On the huge numbers of young Jewish women who became apostates in the eighteenth and nineteenth centuries see Me'ir Balaban, *Le-toledot ha-tenu'ah ha-frankit* [On the history of the Frankist movement], vol. 1. Tel Aviv: Devir, 1934, 92. Balaban noted

alternative, in unusual situations, a boy or young man who wanted no part of the community's expectations regarding matchmaking, marriage, or childrearing could estrange himself from society and choose the mystical path of *devekut* and isolation. To be sure, that option was not well received with regard to men who "craved Torah" in a community that sanctified the commandment to reproduce, but it at least existed in special cases for men. For women, that course was absolutely forbidden and entirely unavailable, and the dybbuk stories mentioned above[68] about women who wanted to stay unmarried and to devote their life to study, but were labeled as possessed by their family male members, demonstrate this point quite clearly.[69]

An-sky, who wrote of himself that "the joy and the tragedy of my life are in my living more in a vision than in reality," examined in depth the bitter fate of those unable to fight back against a social order imposed on them. *The Dybbuk* is based on a rich literary and folkloric tradition[70] that

---

that between the years 1737 and 1820 more than two thousand Jewish women converted to Christianity in Lithuania as a response to a Christian initiative in Vilna known as the Union of Maria. From folktales and dybbuk stories we know that this phenomenon was connected at least partially to the fact that apostasy was perceived as a refuge from coerced sexual relations and arranged marriages.

[68] See n. 63 above.

[69] On ascetic isolation on the part of women in the Jewish world, see Elior, *Nokheḥot nifkadot* (above, n. 7), 227, n. 6; on the same in the non-Jewish world, see Daniel Boyarin, *Carnal Israel: Reading Sex in Talmudic Culture* (Berkeley: Univ. of California Press, 1993), 66–67. On male ascetic isolation in the Jewish tradition, see id., index, s.v. "Rabbinic Judaism, ascetic sexuality"; Steven D. Fraade, "Ascetical Aspects of Ancient Judaism," in Arthur Green, ed., *Jewish Spirituality* 1. New York: Crossroad, 1986, 253–288; David Biale, *Eros and the Jews* (above, n. 4), index, s.v. "celibacy."

[70] In the visitors' book at the Strashun Library in Vilna, An-sky registered the following comment: "The central pillars of our four-thousand-year-old culture are

shows the force of the psychological stress associated with the objects of social domination and regulation, incorporating obvious and latent relationships between strong and weak, rulers and ruled, men and women. An-sky expressed these complex tensions through a play about bodies and souls who, precluded from uniting in this world, employ the means of death, illness, dybbuk, and madness to escape the realm of routine life and its conventional ordering. By means of the dybbuk, they are released from the *devekut* of an imposed match and become able to attain their longed-for union beyond the bounds of time and place.

As noted, Bialik translated An-sky's play from Yiddish to Hebrew in 1917; the translation was published in *Ha-tekufah* in December 1917–January 1918. The play contains an important allusion to the ancient mystical story about the heavenly ascent known as "the four sages who entered paradise [or the grove of mystical Torah study and suffered varied fates, only one emerging unscathed]." (*Tosefta Ḥagigah* 2:3; Bavli *Ḥagigah* 15a–b). One of the four, the *tanna* (mishnaic rabbi) Simeon ben Azzai, is said to have "glanced [at the divine splendor] and died." Khónon is studying that story, engaged in ecstatic yearning and mystical exposition, and dies while in ecstatic union with the divine realm. At that moment, the Messenger announces dramatically, in the wording of the mystical story, "he glanced and died." (*Bein shnei olamot* [Between Two Worlds], Hebrew

---

strong enough to withstand the attacks of any inquisition, whatever it may be. The key is the soul of the nation, which is immortal. A glowing spark of that soul can be sensed here, in the great treasury of books within this building." See Ze'evi-Weill, "*Ha-ḥippus aḥar ha-temimut ha-avudah*" [The search for lost innocence], in *Back to the Shtetl* (above, n. 64), 18. For a survey of the varied literary and folkloric traditions used by An-sky, see Werses, "*Bein shenei olamot*" (above, n. 64).

version,[71] *Ha-tekufah*, 1917–1918, 250). At or about the same time and in the same context, apparently in late 1915 or early 1916, Bialik composed his well known poem "*Heẓiẓ va-met*" ("He glanced and died"), also alluding to the same story.[72] In the image of Khónon, the deceased beloved in An-sky's play whose soul yearned for Torah, as well as in the figure of the protagonist in Bialik's poem, one can see explicit allusions to ben Azzai, who said of himself "My soul yearns for Torah; let the world be

---

[71] In the English translation of S. An-sky, *The Dybbuk and Other Writings*, ed. and with an introduction by David G. Roskies, translations by Golda Werman (New York: Schocken Books, 1992), 20, the verse is translated insensitively to the original mystical context as: "He has been damaged – beyond repair." In the Neugroschel translation (above, n. 51, 21), the line is "He's been destroyed by the demons!"

[72] Bialik did not date "*Heiẓiẓ va-met*"; its timing may be inferred from two dated poems published with it: "*Eḥad eḥad u-ve-ein ro'eh*" (Marḥeshvan 5676 [late 1915]) and "*Ḥalefah al panai*" (Nisan 5676 [spring of 1916]). The three poems were published in volume 1 of *Knesset* in 5677 (1916–1917). See Ḥayyim Naḥman Bialik, *Shirim 5659–5694* (Poems 1898–1934), critical edition ed. by Dan Meron et al. Tel Aviv: Katz Institute for the Study of Hebrew Literature, Tel Aviv University and Dvir, 1990, 352. The editors' introduction to the poem (id.) sees resemblances between the poem and Bialik's article "*Gilui ve-khisui ba-lashon*" (The revealed and the hidden in language), written in October 1915, and the talmudic passage in BT *Ḥagigah* 14b next discussed. On the version of "*Heiẓiẓ va-met*" that states "5676" at its conclusion, see "*Kitvei Hayyim Naḥman Bialik, sefer rishon, shirim: mizmorim u-fizmonot, shirot* (The writings of Ḥayyim Naḥman Bialik, volume 1, Poems…), Tel Aviv: Dvir, 1935, 184–185. On the poem "*Heẓiẓ va-met,*" see Joseph Dan, "'*Heẓiẓ va-met,*'" in *Ha-nokhri ve-ha-mandarin* (The stranger and the mandarin) Ramat Gan: Masada, 1975, 160–166; Barukh Kurzweil, "'*Heẓiẓ va-met*' *le-Bialik ka-hatimah le-shirat ha-yahid*" [Bialik's "*Heẓiẓ va-met*" as the end of individual poetry], in *Bialik ve-Tcherniḥovsky – meḥkarim be-shiratam* (Bialik and Tchernikhovsky – studies in their poetry). Jerusalem and Tel Aviv: Schocken Books, 1961, 146–169; Hillel Barzel, "'*Heẓiẓ va-met*': *ha-mashma'ut ha-alumah*" ("*Heẓiẓ va-met*": the hidden meaning), *Bikkoret u-farshanut* 22 (1986): 15–36.

built by others" (*Yevamot* 62b). Known for his pietistic ways, withdrawal from the world and strict asceticism, ben Azzai died ascending to the upper worlds in mystical exaltation – "he glanced and died," as the Messenger says of Khónon. In his poem, Bialik depicts ben Azzai's ecstatic ascent to the higher worlds as the highest expression of *devekut*. In An-sky's play, the erotic yearnings of the couple who have been arbitrarily separated are resolved by the dybbuk (the spirit of the deceased Khónon clinging to the possessed Leah), which connects the mad bride to the dead groom. In contrast, Bialik presents the figure of the holy ascetic who craves Torah and has no use for erotic attachments in the terrestrial world and yearns only to attain *devekut* in the supernal worlds.

In entering the grove, glancing, and dying, ben Azzai left this world behind, unwilling to participate in building it through physical union and reproduction (*Yevamot* 62b).[73] He did so in order that he might enter "the fiftieth gate;" attain unity with the heavenly embodiment of the supernal Torah, the exalted *Shekhinah*; and bond with the *sefirah* of *binah* (understanding), called *olam ha-ḥerut* (the world of freedom), in the higher worlds.[74] This depiction of separation from the world and mystical

---

[73] On the relationship between spiritual perfection, bound up with love of Torah, and physical asceticism – a relationship that considers this sort of *devekut* in the context of the story of Ben Azzai – see Fraade, "Ascetical Aspects" (above, n. 69), 34, 36, 47. Boyarin alleges Bialik to have been a blatant misogynist (*Carnal Israel* [above, n. 69], 96, n. 29), but he does not make a persuasive case for that view, which is inconsistent with accounts of Bialik's life. Still, Bialik's choice of Ben-Azzai – the archetypical celibate holy man in rabbinic literature, whose spiritual elitism and physical asceticism were opposed by the sages – as the hero of "*Heẓiẓ va-met*" gives one pause.

[74] On "the fiftieth gate" – the prize sought by the hero of "*Heẓiẓ va-met*" even though it was denied to Moses himself and related in kabbalistic literature to the *sefirot* of *binah* (understanding) and *malkhut* (sovereignty) and to the exalted

elevation – known in antiquity as "entering the grove," "entering Paradise," "ascent in the seven sanctuaries" or "descent in the chariot" and in the Middle Ages and early modern times as *devekut* and "union" – is based on the tradition of the divine chariot (1 Chron. 28:18).[75] Ascent to the heavenly realm, which is conditioned on withdrawal from society, isolation, and asceticism, is linked to the account of one who contemplated the divine chariot in order to ascend to the higher worlds and thereby depart from this world. Bialik's poem reflects various traditions that tell of entering paradise and glimpsing the heavenly sanctuaries and that describe Ben Azzai's ascent: his glimpse of the pure marble stones proved too much for his body to bear, and he died. In *Hekhalot zutrati*, we read:

> R. Akiva said: Four of us entered the grove. One glanced and died; one glanced and was injured; one cut the plants

Shekhinah – see Joseph Gikatilla, *Gates of Light* (*Sha'arei orah*), trans. with an introduction by Avi Weinstein, with a foreword by Arthur Hertzberg and an historical introduction by Moshe Idel. San Francisco: Harper Collins, 1994, 283–285, 287–288, 296–297, 302–303. The term was derived from the rabbinic comment that "fifty gates of understanding were created in the world" (Bavli *Rosh ha-Shanah* 21b). In *Sha'arei orah*, Gikatilla sets forth the erotic underpinnings of *devekut*: "Do not be concerned over what the Sages said: 'Is it possible for one to cleave to the Shekhinah?'… and this is the essence of the cleaving of the tenth sefirah to the ninth, without a doubt. For whenever anyone causes the unity of the people of Israel with the sefirah of *yesod, yesod* cleaves to the Shekhinah, and she cleaves to Him and both of them are cleaving to YHVH" (291–292). "… the sefirah binah, which is sometimes called the World to Come. And it is called Yovel, for it is from there that one is freed from bondage to redemption… and from darkness to great light. The essence of Binah is also called Yovel, for in it everyone becomes free…. This Sphere is also called by Kabbalists the *Shekinah Ila'ah* (the supernal *Shekhinah*)" (299–303; 308).

[75] See Elior, *The Three Temples*, 63–80, 232–265.

> [apostatized]… and these are the ones who entered Paradise: Ben Azzai, Ben Zoma, Aḥer ["the other one," a euphemism for Elisha ben Abuyah, who apostatized], and R. Akiva. Ben Azzai glimpsed the sixth heavenly sanctuary and saw the glow of the marble stones with which the sanctuary was paved, but his body could not bear it. He opened his mouth and asked them, "What is the nature of this water?" and then died; of him Scripture says "Precious in the sight of the Lord is the death of His pious ones" (Ps. 116:15).[76]

In "*Heẓiẓ va-met*," Bialik portrays the essence of mystical *devekut* and the associated withdrawal from the world, as it takes place in the life of the ascetic-mystic who strives to cling to the *Shekhinah* and to dedicate his soul to attaining *devekut* beyond the bounds of time and space. In contrast, An-sky sought to depict a dybbuk grasping a flesh-and-blood bride (Leah) who longed for her beloved (Khónon), whose soul had departed in *devekut*, just like Ben Azzai's, and bonded with its deceased partner in order to annul the dominion of the living groom (Menashe) within the bounds of time and space.

An-sky's play cast the dybbuk phenomenon in an entirely new light. Until then, Jewish dybbuk narratives had all been written by authors who had presented the events from a traditional point of view – that of the exorcist, who had come to reinforce the existing order, to strengthen the normative power relationships within the hierarchic, patriarchal society, to

---

[76] *Hekhalot Zutarti (The Lesser Sanctuaries),* ed Rachel Elior. Jerusalem: 1982, 23, 62. On the various contexts and versions of the story of the four who entered Paradise, see Judah Liebes, *Ḥet'o shel Elisha: arba'ah she-nikhnesu la-pardes ve-tiv'ah shel ha-mistikah ha-talmudit* (Elisha's sin: four who entered paradise, and the nature of talmudic mysticism). Jerusalem: Hebrew University, 1986; Rachel Elior, *The Three Temples,* 232–265.

assign sacred force to the norm, and to restore stability. These writers, sometimes themselves exorcists or officials of the community within which the ceremony was conducted, aimed to tell of the lot of those who challenged the prevailing order. To do so, they depicted the fate of the driven spirit that forces itself on the possessed woman but ultimately is expelled by the communal official – the representative of sound order based on dominion and obedience, mastery and coercion.

An-sky, however, reveals the complexity of the encounter between worlds by describing it from the unexpected perspective of soulmates whose loving desire for each other undermines a coerced match – the perspective of a bride and groom denied the opportunity to marry but ultimately joining in death beyond the bounds of time and space. The dybbuk, by the power of madness, transfers the bride and groom to another world, transcends them from the world of the living to the world of the dead, thereby liberating the bride from a union she does not want and allowing her to unite with her longed-for mate who entered paradise or engaged in the ecstatic life of *devekut.*

When asked "Who are you?" Khónon, the dybbuk, responds through Leah's throat, "I am one of those who looked for new paths." Bialik's poem describes an ascetic hero yearning for his eternal celestial love – the *sefirah* of *binah*, the supernal Torah, or the exalted *Shekhinah* – which he seeks to attain through paths that lead beyond the bounds of time and space:

> He continued striving, and found
> the straightest way –
> crooked way.
> Going along it, he came

to a time and place –
of no time and no place.[77]

In both contexts, the word *shevilim* (rendered as "paths" in Neugroschel's translation of the play and as "way" in Barzel's translation of the poem) is used in describing the struggles between the worlds; the word recalls the comment of the *amora* (post-mishnaic talmudic rabbi) Samuel that "the paths of heaven are as clear to me as the paths of Nehardea (his town)" (*Berakhot* 51b). Both texts also sought to describe the passageways between the worlds and to show the proximity between two sorts of *devekut*: on the one hand, *devekut* and devotion formulated as "he glimpsed inside, and his body dropped… and stretched itself on the threshold of *Belimah*"[78] (said of ben Azzai in Bialik's poem); on the other, a bonding in which a soul denied terrestrial union (Khónon) departs the world in longing for *devekut* with the *Shekhinah* and the *sefirah* of *binah*, the domain of freedom, only to return reincarnated in a different body (Leah) as a dybbuk that removes the person so possessed from the bounds of the social order. In both instances, the hero's fate is accompanied by a fire going out: in ben Azzai's case, the poet says, "Then the torch expired."[79] In Khónon's case, the Messenger's line, following Khónon's collapse, is "The candle has burned down, I must light a new one."[80]

---

[77] Translation by Hillel Barzel, in Hillel Barzel and Stephen Katz, "The Concealed Meaning of Ḥayyim Naḥman Bialik's 'He Glimpsed and Died.'" *Modern Language Studies* 19/3 (Summer 1989): 26–49, at 26.

[78] Id., 27.

[79] Id.

[80] Neugroschel, *The Dybbuk and the Yiddish Imagination* (above, n. 54), 20. For a scholarly update on An-sky's work see: Steven Zipperstein and Gabriella Safran, eds. *The Worlds of An- sky, A Russian Jewish Intellectual on the Turn of the Century.* Stanford: Stanford University Press, 2006.

I have sought here to round out the perspective afforded by the traditional dybbuk narratives. Those narratives, written in a hegemonic voice, reflected the values of the community and served the clear didactic purpose of bolstering the traditional order and illustrating it through a story and conceptual system presenting the conventional view of the truth. I have added the perspective of those who could not find their place within the traditional social order and, seeking liberation from it, were characterized as possessed by a dybbuk or by *devekut*. I have also attempted to examine the perspective of those possessed by a dybbuk – to evoke their silenced voices and explain the circumstances underlying the proliferation of women possessed by dybbuks who were afflicted by hysteria and madness in the traditional patriarchal world and in its modern-day manifestations. Physical and mental illnesses lend themselves to different interpretations by those who maintain the norm and those subject to it, by those invested with medical authority and those considered to be ill, and even by those who establish the conventional interpretations. Like any other social discourse, the dialogue among these voices draws on novel insights, changes in power relationships, and altered critical and interpretive postures. The boundary lines between past and present are more obscure with regard to social history in general and relations between the sexes in particular than they are with regard to other areas of history. That is because intellectual, interpretive, and behavioral rubrics, as well as linguistic coinages, bind past and present together by the reins of tradition. But with a broadened range of perspectives from which to examine past and present comes an improved ability to appreciate properly the complexity of the reality memorialized in language – a reality until recently regarded in many circles as self-evident yet one that poses, from the perspective of our own times, difficult questions indeed.

Index